INDEPENDENT PRACTICE FOR THE MENTAL HEALTH PROFESSIONAL

T0139330

INDEPENDENT PRACTICE FOR THE MENTAL HEALTH PROFESSIONAL

Growing a Private Practice for the 21st Century

by
Ralph H. Earle, Ph.D., A.B.P.P.
Dorothy J. Barnes, M.C., N.C.C.

 Routledge
Taylor & Francis Group

LONDON AND NEW YORK

INDEPENDENT PRACTICE FOR THE MENTAL HEALTH PROFESSIONAL:
Growing a Private Practice for the 21st Century

First published 1999 by BRUNNER/MAZEL

Published 2014 by Routledge
2 Park Square, Milton Park, Abingdon, Oxfordshire OX14 4RN
711 Third Avenue, New York , NY 10017

First issued in paperback 2014
Routledge is an imprint of the Taylor & Francis Group an informa business

Cover design by Claire O'Neill.

A CIP catalog record for this book is available from the British Library.

Library of Congress Cataloging-in-Publication Data available from Publisher.

ISBN 978-0-876-30838-7 (hbk)
ISBN 978-1-138-00502-0 (pbk)

CONTENTS

PREFACE

- Therapists must realize that the days of private-practice therapy are limited.
- Increasing numbers of recent graduates work for large health-maintenance organizations with starting pay equal to a beginning teacher's salary.
- Therapists are very compassionate, but they're lousy business managers.
- Managed care has grown so much that it completely dominates the mental-health service available.

Around every corner in the mental-health world these days is someone more than willing to predict the imminent demise of private practice. The comments at the start of this Preface can be overheard at seminars, workshops, and gathering places in which therapists discuss the current and future state of their profession.

As we revise this book, we are acutely aware of how rapidly the health-care world is changing day-by-day. Changes in delivery systems portend other changes as well. The public demands answers to questions about their stretched-to-the-limits pocketbooks and decreasing choices about their mental and physical well-being. Different views and predictions about the changes in our healthcare system continue to bombard the mental-health practitioner. There is a new healthcare proposal around every political corner, and the current system seems to be challenged on a regular basis. The eventual outcome is sure to affect all types of health services including the mental-health field.

Some professionals think our healthcare system will continue to grow more stratified, resulting in a system similar to that in England: nationalized, social healthcare with a small number of private doctors for the very few who can afford them. Others think that our U.S. system may develop more tiers—private care, private care with insurance reimbursement, semi-private care through HMOs and PPOs, nationalized care for the indigent, and little to no care for the "notch" group (that is, those who do not qualify for indigent care but cannot afford or are not eligible for other forms of care)—but that the effects of the system will be similar: The number of therapists able to be supported in private practice under this system will be greatly diminished.

While the debate continues, the professional therapist in private practice must traverse the maze while making future decisions about uncertain outcomes. Learning to live and work within the ambiguities of the profession presents a challenge and an opportunity for the independent practitioner.

Various arguments have been given to support the differing viewpoints about our healthcare system and its future revision. We have witnessed the growth and placement of "alphabet soup" organizations (HMOs, PPOs, EAPs, etc.) designed to contain costs and provide management for healthcare providers. Private practice has experienced rising costs in malpractice and professional liability insurance, rising administrative and overhead costs, and rising fee schedules that some feel will price private practitioners out of the market. Another factor contributing to the uncertainty about the mental-health field is the sheer proliferation of mental-health practitioners with varying degrees and kinds of professional training and certification. Redefinition of therapy itself, especially the increasing emphasis on brief therapy, also has contributed to these predictions.

Why then this book, if private practice, now on the endangered-species list according to most prognosticators, is destined for extinction in the near future?

We believe, in spite of dire warnings, that private practice is here to stay. In fact, our prediction is that the 21st century will present exciting opportunities in private practice not available to us before. These opportunities will not be restricted to any traditional group of practitioners (for example, psychiatrists or psychologists) and, in fact, will widen in scope for many types of professionals. Therapists need to adapt to the changing marketplace in order to avail themselves of these opportunities.

There is one catch: The opportunities most likely will be there for *those who are willing to conceive creatively of themselves as both therapists and businesspeople.* Those in private practice will need to accept the fact that what they do is both a service and a business.

Many therapists, however, have a difficult time accepting this premise. If we were to ask therapists, including those in private practice, if they offer an important "product"—namely, therapy—they would first balk at using the word "product" and then answer yes to the question. Often these same therapists contradict their own assessment of therapy's worth by refusing to take seriously the business of providing it.

We can explain some of this antipathy by looking back at what appealed to us about practicing therapy in the first place.

Ralph Earle:

It is clear to me after practicing therapy full-time since 1971 that the business side of my life has never been a main motivation in career choice for me. One of the first choices I made regarding being in a helping profession was whether to be a teacher of religion or to go into the parish ministry. I chose to be a parish minister. From that choice evolved the decision to become a therapist; I worked in different settings and finally ended up in private practice.

The real adrenaline rush for me professionally is to see people's lives actually change through the process of therapy. Everybody's journey in becoming a therapist is different, and I have learned to be thankful for my own. I have never regretted the choice to be a therapist full-time, and continue to realize there are more options to exercise in private practice than time left for me to follow the myriad of choices.

Dorothy Barnes:

I chose a career in counseling so I could work with people who needed help sorting out and working through problem areas. Prior to becoming a counselor I had been in sales, administrative work, and several educational programs that involved service to others, such as teaching and audiology. Nothing seemed to fit. Working with people through my other career choices eventually helped define the type of interaction I wanted to have with others in my career. Eventually I went through my own therapy process, and a spark of desire was ignited that never went out. The human experience is fragile and resilient at the same time. I love the opportunity of standing with someone in her or his darkest and lightest moments.

In other words, we did not become therapists in order to be businesspeople. What we soon realized was that it was crucial for us to see ourselves as businesspeople and therapists in order to survive and succeed. One of the premises of this book is that, if you really believe in the value of therapy in the private practice setting, the "business" of therapy does not have to be odious or conducted according to a set of values different from the ones you follow in the practice of therapy, or in your personal life.

This is a book about growing a private practice and is relevant for new and established clinicians. It is about seeing what you do—the therapy and the business—as a whole. It is about strategies for success that involve knowing who you are and capitalizing on that knowledge. This book is not a how-to manual in the traditional sense. What color to paint your walls, what kind of ads to run in the yellow pages, and what structure is best for a private practice are personal decisions. This book is a guide to help you formulate those decisions and move through to a new way of thinking about yourself and your practice.

We think it is important to understand who you are in relation to practice building. Part I, on personal identity, helps you assess what kind of person you are in terms of operating in a private practice setting. We think that making a private practice work demands a thorough assessment of your capabilities and desires, to be in a business by yourself or with a group of independent practitioners.

Certainly some personality characteristics more readily lend themselves to the nuances of private practice, and others may be less effective. Unless there is a side of you that likes to get out (that is, to meet people, to put yourself in different situations and look at them from innovative angles) and create new avenues for your practice, then private practice probably is not the ideal arena for you.

Remember, however, that not all private practices are alike. You may not be the type of person who wants to get out enough to make a solo practice work. Sharing a practice with a person who enjoys practice building to the point of generating enough referrals for both of you (while you take primary responsibility for some other aspect of the practice) may be the perfect arrangement for you. Building a group practice in which different specialties and business expertise are brought together as a cohesive unit certainly can be helpful when going into the private sector. The scenarios and settings for independent practice are as varied as the type of professionals in them.

In Chapter 2 we offer portraits of professionals currently in private practice. Through the eyes of others you can begin to sense the diversity and opportunity that await any therapist who wants to be in private practice.

Remember, too, that life stages interact with personality. Someone in his or her 20s, recently graduated from school, experiences unique challenges in building a private practice. This person must possess or obtain practice-building skills that other practitioners already might have gained through life experience and prior careers. A partnership with a therapist who already has practice-building expertise, and who wants to join with a new member of the profession, could be profitable and rewarding for both.

This same person, however, in his or her 30s or 40s may have established enough connections in the community to succeed without investing an inordinate amount of time in seeking knowledge about practice-building activities and skills. Some other people in their 50s and 60s may have established so great a reputation that only minimal practice-building activities are necessary. Others in this age group might want to establish only a small, part-time practice to supplement retirement income from other sources.

There is an increasing trend toward multiple careers in a lifetime. Counseling and private practice are possibilities for the entrepreneur, business owner, or corporate manager who decides to change careers. Those professionals bring a wealth of business knowledge with them to the field of counseling.

Ideas and beliefs about success, changes in those ideas over time, personality, and life stage all influence a person's ability to develop a successful private practice. Your definition of what it means to be successful will influence the amount and kind of practice building you need to do.

It is our thinking, borne out in workshop and personal experience, that most therapists have practice-building sides to themselves. They simply have not tapped into them because they have not developed models for building businesses based on their own identities and lifestyles. It is not because they do not want to but rather because no one has taught them how to do it. So, although this book is not a traditional how-to book, it is a training or retraining book to help you think about the business of private practice in a way in which you may not have thought of it before.

In this sense the book is participatory. Throughout the book are exercises to help you assess how best to create, build, and maintain your private practice. The questions are open-ended; there are no right or wrong answers, no scores to tally up your chances of succeeding in private practice. The importance of any of these exercises or sample forms we provide is determined by their usefulness to you. To this end, we also have tried to avoid being overly directive. We talk a lot about our own experiences, because we want you to see how what we do is based on who we are, and to begin thinking about what you can do based on who you are.

We offer many examples of therapists in private practice and how they view the nature and scope of their service to others. Reading about how others operate and define their therapy practice can help you do the same. It is our hope that the examples offer encouragement and can stimulate your own creativity in building a practice that suits your needs and desires.

The words "private practice" certainly are not meant to suggest that you stay private in what you are doing—that you do not tell anyone, nor that your clients do not tell anyone (client and patient are used interchangeably throughout the book to reflect different usages by therapists). Soon you would have no practice about which to stay private.

We all have heard the injunction against starting too many sentences with "I"; it is not "nice" to talk about yourself. The training of therapists, although not so discouraging as past warnings against revealing personal information to a client, certainly has not gone to the other extreme of "go ahead and talk all you want about yourself." Nor do we think it should. The effect of this training, however, is that as therapists we are uncomfortable revealing ourselves to clients, although clients represent one of our primary sources of referrals.

Part II, on public identity, is devoted to helping you to devise ways to market yourself and your practice effectively. Chapter 3 discusses some of the resistances we may have toward marketing ourselves and provides a model for cooperation rather than competition. Chapter 3 closes with a discussion of ideas about success and how they influence practice building. Chapter 4 helps you take your private practice public. We suggest ways to develop a marketing plan to help you build your practice. We reflect our differing stages of career building, with Ralph being the senior career person, who started his career in 1971, and Dorothy, at the time of this writing, just beginning private practice as a therapist. Chapter 5 explains exactly how to develop a marketing plan to help you build your practice. We close the chapter with a discussion of the relationship between specializing in a particular aspect of mental-health practice and marketing your practice. Chapter 6 examines various types of large healthcare organizations, detailing the many opportunities for affiliation that these organizations present to the independent practitioner who wants to remain independent. Finally, Chapter 7 takes a look at managed care and how it affects private practice.

The principles and strategies that we outline in this book are applicable to all therapists: psychologists, marital and family therapists, social workers, professional counselors, psychiatric nurses, psychiatrists, pastoral counselors, and so on. One of the points we emphasize is that therapists need to develop both their professional and business effectiveness, and that effectiveness in these areas is not necessarily a function of the academic degree a person has.

One of the benefits of managed care has been the breakdown of barriers between healthcare professionals. There has been an increased utilization of Master's-level therapists throughout the counseling community. So-called turf wars between professionals have decreased, and the need for growth and expansion in all sectors of the counseling arena has increased.

To complement the emphasis on marketing effectiveness, Part III, on business and professional identity, deals with developing business and professional effectiveness and discusses issues you need to consider in order to run your independent practice as a successful small business. Chapter 8 discusses the pros and cons of various types of independent practice such as solo and group practice. Chapter 9 helps you determine the physical characteristics of your office (location, design, furnishings, and so on) that best reflect the kind of practice you want. We raise some issues that you as an employer of support personnel need to consider. In this chapter, we also discuss issues of setting and collecting fees (including third-party reimbursement) and suggest practices that make these tasks easier and less traumatic for both therapist and patient.

Finally, we provide some guidelines for your business and personal financial planning. The first part of Chapter 10 discusses three legal issues—confidentiality, dual relationships, and negligence—that should be of increasing concern to all mental-health practitioners because of the proliferation of litigation in these areas in recent years. The second part of the chapter deals with strategies you can use to help protect yourself against legal liability.

Again—we cannot emphasize this point enough—our purpose is not to tell you how to do it, but rather to suggest new ways of thinking that allow you to create or recreate yourself as a functioning, energized human being. In this particular context, developing a successful independent practice in mental-health services is the focus. However, the principles we discuss can be applied to any number of independent ventures. Our business is not different from any other business, including the need for moral values that extend beyond the bottom line. If this book helps you to both define your moral values and goals and incorporate them into the creation, growth, and maintenance of your independent practice, then we have done our job.

ACKNOWLEDGMENTS

We would like to give most special thanks to Joan Beigel whose lifestyle choices have led her to decide that this update of *Successful Private Practice in the 1990s* should be completed without her direct input. However, the original manuscript would never have seen the light of day without her expertise, excitement, and willingness to help make that dream a reality. With her permission and blessing we have brought together the past, present, and future for a successful independent practice for the 21st century.

We also would like to thank those who contributed their expertise to this book: Marcus Earle, Marilyn Murray, Nicholas Cummings, James Butcher, and Steven Engelberg.

Additional thanks are extended to the staff at Brunner/Mazel who collaborated to publish the first edition and have now joined with the Taylor & Francis Publishing House. Taylor & Francis have adopted the book, and us as authors, to bring you *Independent Practice for the Mental Health Professional.*

For manuscript help and editing we want to thank Karen Wise and Marsha Sherer, whose attention to detail and willingness to help successfully moved the manuscript to completion.

Finally, we would like to thank our families and friends whose love, support, and encouragement help sustain and energize us through the "projects" of our lives.

PRIVATE PRACTICE AND PERSONAL IDENTITY

Define Yourself to Define Your Practice

Independent practice for the mental-health professional means different lifestyles, personalities, and practices. Therapists in private practice design their careers in ways that usually are not available to therapists in other settings. This freedom constitutes one of the main motivations for going into independent practice. Although the designs may look different, the common thread is choice.

An alignment takes place when a therapist enters private practice. Personal and professional identities come together as part of the marketing package needed for an independent professional to thrive. Personalities, styles of therapy practiced, and business personas become congruent.

To be successful in private practice, you need to know and understand your own personality and motivations for being an independent practitioner. There are a variety of personality characteristics that can contribute to success in a business venture of any type. Certain traits seem to lend themselves to being able to function in private versus community-agency settings.

It is our experience, however, that personality type is most relevant in determining *how* you will structure your marketing and business time, as opposed to *whether* you are suited for private practice. By defining who you are you can consciously choose a business strategy that allows you to stay in private practice, resist burnout, and get what you want from the business of doing therapy.

☐ The Helper and the Entrepreneur

How do you develop that congruence between self and practice? The independent practitioner lives at least two major roles: helper and entrepreneur. What are the stereotypic traits associated with success in each role? Stop now and create two lists. Title the first list "The Traits And Stereotypes Of A Helping Professional." Name the other "The Traits And Stereotypes You Associate With An Entrepreneur." Take some time and write down any label or trait that comes to mind for each list. This exercise can be used in a group setting and often is enlightening and entertaining.

Compare the lists you created with the lists we present below. The following lists are a composite of the responses we have received through workshops, seminars, and conversations with other professionals.

Helper	Entrepreneur
receptive	aggressive
objective	persuasive
process-directed	product-directed
altruistic	materialistic
female	male
yin	yang
people-centered	market-centered
educated	streetwise
introverted	extroverted
noble poor	ignoble rich
ethical	unscrupulous
Bambi	Jaws

The problem seems obvious: These two roles are mutually exclusive, equally unrealistic, and in our opinion unfair. We currently are involved in writing a gender book, because it is our experience that male and female roles are often the first hurdles to cross when evaluating effectiveness in many professional settings. Certainly many females are successful entrepreneurs, and many males are effective helping professionals.

Adhering to these stereotypes, while trying to resolve the conflicts inherent in them, is impossible and leads to the failure of many practices and to severe burnout among many practitioners. Belief in these stereotypes is one reason therapists have trouble with areas of their business such as public speaking, setting fees, advertising, or talking about what they do.

Many private-practice therapists have been accused of being "hustlers"—the quintessential entrepreneurial bad person—on the basis of this helper-entrepreneur dichotomy. In his second year of family therapy practice with a group in Scottsdale, Arizona, Ralph received an envelope from the Board of Psychologist Examiners. This is not the kind of mail a therapist wants to receive under any circumstances, but certainly not when he or she is new in town and just beginning a practice. Inside the envelope was a letter that a Phoenix man had sent to the state Board, which stated that Ralph was a hustler and documented the man's unhappiness with Ralph's behavior. The Board wanted Ralph to let them know what had happened from his point of view. He replied, and then they sent a letter to the man that indicated that what Ralph had done was standard operating procedure and not a problem. Some of Ralph's friends told him, "He was really giving you a compliment."

Although Dorothy, being new to the profession, has not yet received the brand of "hustler," she has noticed her reluctance to talk about fees and a tendency to go as low on a sliding scale as the patient deems necessary. One client asked for a greatly reduced fee due to a divorce and current shortage of assets and funds. The sessions went on for a time, and the continuing theme of "no money" continued. During a group session the client forgot his declaration of poverty and admitted to having a great deal of money and assets. Dorothy's fear of being considered a "hustler" led to her shortchanging her own practice.

One of the first areas with which you must come to terms when entering private practice is the issue of money. There is no single right way to do therapy, and there is no single right way to determine business practice for doing therapy. We, Dorothy and Ralph, choose an approach or some mixture of approaches based on context: our own personalities, our training and experience, the patient's personality, and our assessment of the problem at a particular time. Likewise, there is no single right way to conduct business. We choose activities and strategies based on context: our own personalities, our training and experience, our market, and our goal at a particular time. Notice that training and experience appear in both lists.

When therapists join Ralph's practice, Psychological Counseling Services (PCS), they often say, "I'm trained in [whatever style of therapy], or at least feel most comfortable there." There is never any mention of training in the business of independent practice. Most therapists are very comfortable with the kind of therapy they do because they are well trained. They are not comfortable with the idea of running a business because they have received no training, unless they come from a business background. In our opinion, it requires more than just therapeutic technique to make a business successful, whether in an office behind closed doors or in public.

☐ The Independent Practice "Personality"

We include here a dialogue between us, discussing our ideas of qualities or characteristics that we think are important in independent practice. This dialogue is meant to encourage you to have a similar dialogue with others in the field, as a means of beginning to define your ideas about private practice. In Chapter 2 we present portraits of professionals who are currently in private practice. Here we give you our own perspectives, with Ralph as a senior independent-practice therapist and Dorothy as a junior independent-practice therapist.

Listening In

Ralph (R): *Dorothy, as a therapist just embarking on a career in counseling, what qualities do you think are important for somebody in independent practice?*

Dorothy (D): *Flexibility and creativity come to mind.*

R: *Flexibility and creativity—both good words and necessary qualities. Flexibility and creativity are needed for the business and the clinical sides of independent practice.*

D: *Ralph, I'm curious about the qualities you look for when thinking about hiring a therapist to be part of your practice at PCS.*

R: *Self-motivation is essential for all therapists, and it becomes especially important to me when I'm thinking about hiring someone. Motivation dictates whether or not a person will provide her or his own clients, along with the clients that come from others in the practice.*

D: *It seems to me that motivation is a quality that has to come with the person, and probably cannot be taught.*

R: *Historically, I've been unsuccessful teaching someone to have motivation if they do not already have that when they come into our practice. In fact, probably the most frustrating part of administering a group practice for me has been to try to teach someone, who may be a very capable therapist, to be motivated to do the work it takes to build a practice.*

D: *For me it has been important to determine my motivational level in order to help me make decisions about time spent in both building my practice and the types of activities to pursue.*

R: *That's a great point. Another quality that seems to be important is having autonomy to make decisions. I enjoy working with people who really do have a great deal of autonomy and are not reliant on me or others to make basic decisions.*

D: *Working as an intern at PCS, and later as an employee, I was both pleased* *and overwhelmed in the beginning about how many choices I had the freedom to make.*

R: *The learning curve in any new situation certainly applies to being a clinician in a private practice setting. Being an intern in such a setting can be a nonthreatening way to check out the possibility of working as an independent practitioner without the stress of having to secure clients.*

D: *Tell me more about autonomy and how that blends with being a team player.*

R: *Over the years I've understood just how important it is to be a team player if you are working independently with other clinicians. Basically, a person who enjoys being part of a team will find working in a practice such as ours to be very meaningful. A person who may be autonomous and want to work completely alone may do better in a solo setting.*

D: *Who would be an ideal PCS therapist?*

R: *An ideal PCS therapist would be someone who is creating and broadening the scope of ideas, in terms of marketing, and at the same time also becoming an important part of the continuing education of others in the group. Some of the more exciting moments are the sharing of ideas when we are staffing a particular case, and listening to the varied opinions about what type of treatment makes the most sense. There are times when we agree to disagree and learn from each other.*

The ideal person is the person who gets an adrenaline rush from clinical work as well as from marketing. The combination of those two activities are necessary to continue to find independent practice meaningful.

D: *What about ability to organize?*

R: *I see that as a key area in independent practice. I handle a lot of administrative details, but I don't make money by administering. I don't get paid for doing that, and it's not the part I enjoy the most. When I'm on the clock, the patient's needs come first. When I'm off that clock, then I'd rather be playing golf or be with my family or friends. I've noticed that many of the people with whom we've consulted spend a tremendous amount of time obsessing about the business side.*

D: *We haven't mentioned money yet.*

R: *The bottom line is we really have to be willing to ask for payment and expect it. My experience is that frequently therapists at the beginning of private practice undervalue themselves in many ways including what they are worth.*

D: *Are there any other qualities we need to mention?*

R: *Freedom and responsibility are two related issues: the freedom to do what you want and the responsibility to do what needs to be done. How you feel about both areas will influence the way you structure your independent practice.*

We think that there are other personality characteristics that contribute to success in independent practice. Creating an independent practice in the first place takes confidence; confidence also is required to do what you need to do to build the practice, which is going to involve risk and the unknown. If you are not confident about both your therapeutic and business abilities, you will have a difficult time succeeding in independent practice. One way you can confront your anxiety is by attending workshops or seminars that deal with business issues. (You may already be confronting your anxiety by reading this book!) Another way is to find someone else in your field in your locality whom you think is successful and buy supervision time from him or her.

Many of these business-anxiety issues are therapy issues. For instance, if you are not allowed to be successful, you are not allowed to make money. It is important to work through anxiety in an effort to align these personal and professional identities; otherwise, you may do everything right, at least to outward appearances, but you will make yourself so nervous and tense about it, you will wind up sick—and so will your practice.

Here we want to raise a key concept, the notion of appropriateness. We believe that a therapist in private practice must develop a keen sense of values consistent with community and professional standards, whether in behavior, therapeutic practice, dress, community image, or office image.

Balance is a good word on which to focus when exploring appropriateness in private practice. Looking at the extremes in behavior helps describe the balance needed. Behavior outside the clinical setting becomes a major focus of appropriateness. Although it would be nice to think that our behavior during therapy sessions matches our behavior outside of sessions, that is not always the case. It becomes an absolute necessity to be congruent in your behavior when working in private practice. You do begin to live in somewhat of a fishbowl, which can work to your benefit or detriment.

Therapeutic practice must be in line with legal and ethical governing boards, and responsibility for that lies with the independent practitioner. If you work in a large clinical setting, there usually are legal resources available to help you, but you must secure those resources on your own time and money when in private practice.

We receive referrals based upon our therapeutic practice and specialties. Keeping abreast of current theory and technique goes beyond the number of hours necessary for continuing education. It is important for independent practitioners to create an atmosphere of learning and growing in the counseling field.

Dress and community image are other areas in which appropriateness becomes an ongoing issue for therapists in private practice. Here in the

Southwest it is appropriate to wear more casual business attire than back East. Walking into a counseling session or a business-marketing setting with a three-piece suit may or may not be suitable for either the weather or the emotional climate. In order to have a community image you must be involved in your community. (You certainly do not have to worry about an appropriate image if you have no image at all.)

Office image for some professionals can almost be a Jekyll and Hyde personality dichotomy. We all have seen the professional who masquerades as a caring, considerate individual, only to catch a glimpse of him or her interacting with office staff as an intolerant, demanding ogre. Patients have eyes and ears to witness our shadow side when we least expect. Be aware of your behavior, and make changes when necessary.

Flexibility and availability also are key traits that often go together for independent practitioners. Some therapists find it difficult to be in independent practice and not be on 24-hour call. This does not mean that you have to make yourself available to all patients 24 hours a day, 7 days a week, 52 weeks a year. It does mean, however, that you have some system in place to handle emergencies; it means that you arrange with a colleague to cover for you if you want to be free of responsibility for a time; it means that you may have to see a family for the first time late at night or early in the morning.

We have to determine individually the level of our flexibility. Ralph's group practice reflects a variety of work hours among the therapists. A typical schedule for Ralph might look like this:

> Monday, 7:00 a.m.–6:00 p.m.
> Tuesday, 7:00 a.m.–7:30 p.m.
> Wednesday, 7:00 a.m.–6:00 p.m.
> Thursday, 7:00 a.m.–11:00 p.m. (golf in the afternoon)
> Friday, 7:00 a.m.–5:00 p.m.

Dorothy's schedule reflects her mixture of professional writing and counseling:

> Monday, 8:00 a.m.–5:00 p.m., client hours
> Tuesday, 8:00 a.m.–5:00 p.m., client hours
> Wednesday, 7:00 a.m.–12:00 p.m., writing
>   12:00 p.m.–6:00 p.m., client hours
> Thursday, 8:00 a.m.–5:00 p.m., writing
> Friday, 8:00 a.m.–5:00 p.m., client hours

In the early stages of practice building the counseling hours may be equal to the marketing hours. Flexibility means continually looking at your schedule and revising the hours allocated for different activities.

Ralph has always made it a practice to "strike while the iron is hot" when it comes to marketing opportunities:

> I received a call one day from a minister who, with his wife, was doing a marriage-enrichment program that evening at a church. They ended up with 95 couples and were overwhelmed; they wanted to know if I could help. This was the last day I was going to be in town for a while, and I was seeing patients until 6 that evening, but I said that I would do it. I like to take opportunities when they present themselves both in terms of prevention of later problems for those people attending the program, and as a response to a particular person with a need (who also is more likely to become a referral source in the future), as opposed to saying, "I see patients from 7 to 6 and I'll be too tired."

For new and seasoned clinicians in private practice, the need to have new clients never goes away. Some therapists refuse to take on new patients if their case load reaches a certain number. Others continue to accept new clients regardless of the current number of patients that are being seen. Both policies seem to work, and each has drawbacks inherent in the system.

There are, however, limits to us all. The balance for us is to try to do those activities that make the most sense when they become possible. For others, who even may have the same idea about balance, the manifestations may be quite different. It is important that each therapist, whether in group or solo practice, defines the way she or he needs to live out her or his own value system. It is a matter of finding out what is comfortable in your value system, based on where you are in your life stage, what relationship you want with your family and friends, and what you hope to accomplish in your counseling career.

What are the personality traits and characteristics necessary to succeed in independent practice? You have read some of our ideas, but the most pertinent answer to this question from your viewpoint lies with you. The design of your practice, if it is to succeed, must reflect your values, beliefs, personality, and goals.

The therapeutic community is expert in defining these areas. The challenge is in shaping the relationship between you and your business. If we were helping clients in relationship, the first step might be to administer personality tests to them. This is not a bad idea in this relationship. Depending on your preferences and prejudices, you might refer to your own scores on the Minnesota Multiphasic Personality Inventory, the Myers-Briggs Type Indicator Test, the Rorschach, or Performax's Personal Profile System. The information from those tests indicates some stylistic traits. Remember that there is no one way, personality style, or belief system that equals success in private practice. You want to gather information about yourself and shape the business accordingly.

For example, our scores on the Myers-Briggs scale are different. Ralph tends to score high on the Extroversion scale and Dorothy's score falls somewhere on the Introversion scale. Scoring high on the Introversion scale does not mean that you cannot market yourself, or even that the marketing will be difficult. Scoring high on the Extroversion scale would seem to mean success in marketing, although that is not necessarily true either. We both enjoy public speaking, presenting workshops, and trade shows, for instance. Differences are evidenced more in the types of energy and preparation needed, as well as time spent on "alone" types of activities.

We tailored the following questionnaire to help you place yourself and your business in a healthy relationship. Each assessment is meant to bring to your awareness goals, desires, and areas for improvement as you begin to define yourself and your practice.

☐ Self-Assessment

1. List two goals in each of the following categories:

    Personal _____

    _____

    _____

    Significant others _____

    _____

    _____

    Professional _____

    _____

    _____

    Spiritual _____

    _____

    _____

    Humanitarian _____

    _____

    _____

    Playing _____

    _____

    _____

    Other _____

    _____

    _____

2. List two techniques that you are using to accomplish these goals:

Personal_____

_____

_____

Significant others_____

_____

_____

Professional_____

_____

_____

Spiritual_____

_____

_____

Humanitarian_____

_____

_____

Other_____

_____

_____

3. Define your current balance:

Personal_____

_____

_____

Significant others_____

_____

_____

Community_____

_____

_____

Spirituality_____

_____

_____

Professional_____

_____

_____

Playing_____

_____

_____

Other_____

_____

_____

4. What role does your practice play in your ability to reach your goals?

Personal_____

_____

_____

Significant others_____

_____

_____

Professional_____

_____

_____

Spiritual_____

_____

_____

Humanitarian_____

_____

_____

Other_____

_____

_____

5. What role does your practice play in inhibiting your attempts to reach your goals?

Personal_____

_____

_____

Significant others_____

_____

_____

Professional_____

_____

_____

Spiritual_____

_____

_____

Humanitarian_____

_____

_____

Other_____

_____

_____

6. How can you use your professional life to further your goals?

Personal_____

_____

_____

Significant others_____

_____

_____

Professional_____

_____

_____

Spiritual_____

_____

_____

Humanitarian_____

_____

_____

Other_____

_____

_____

7. How can you overcome the ways in which your practice inhibits accomplishment of your goals?

Personal_____

_____

_____

Significant others_____

_____

_____

Professional_____

_____

_____

Spiritual_____

_____

_____

Humanitarian_____

_____

_____

Other_____

_____

_____

8. What personal qualities are required of the independent practitioner?_____

   _____

   _____

9. Which of these qualities do you believe you have?

   _____

   _____

   _____

10. How will these qualities assist you in developing your practice?

    _____

    _____

    _____

11. If you believe that you do not have some of the qualities you have listed, how will you compensate?

    _____

    _____

    _____

12. Comments

    _____

    _____

    _____

☐ Identity and Practice Building

In the end, in analyzing your own personality and needs, you begin almost automatically to start thinking about business not as an adversary (to whom you are hopelessly ill suited), but as a natural extension of your personal identity, including the type of therapy you practice. Because relationship therapy is what we believe in, we see the business end of our practice as relationship-centered, also.

Our business is based on caring, empathizing, and creating rapport. Going back to the old Rogerian tenet, a kind of connectedness can occur in the daily course of life. For example, you run into a neighbor at the nearby dry-cleaning store. When you ask about his family, he mentions that his son in a neighboring city has been having problems. You tell him about a colleague in that city whom you know well and respect. You are not trying to give your neighbor a sales pitch or hustle business for your colleague (or yourself in the form of return referrals); you are attempting to assist a neighbor who has a problem. The connection is a human one between two neighbors, friends, or colleagues.

For the most part, people are not going to decide to see therapists based on where they got their degrees or on what styles of therapy they practice. We sometimes get so sophisticated in our own field that we begin to look at certain aspects as marketable or not marketable, forgetting that when it comes to business, what is in vogue may be irrelevant; it is the relationship that counts.

This same principle underlies the business decisions you make with your colleagues. You care for your colleagues as people and not as production units. You deal with their feelings as well as behavior, taking into account their perceptions and values. Whatever business decisions you make grow from the human connections you establish first.

Balance, Not Burnout

The trick to creating, building, and maintaining an independent practice is to think building and act on these thoughts when opportunities present themselves, without going too far in that direction and becoming a workaholic or a person who cannot refrain from being "on." The inability to balance all the important facets of your life, of which your practice is but one, results in burnout.

If your activities are rooted in your identity, however, and your dealings with people are rooted in the human connections you establish, there is less chance that you will burn yourself out. If what you are doing ceases to be fun—that is, satisfying, energizing, and motivating—and starts to be drudgery, you need to stand back and admit, "This isn't working for me, I've got to make some adjustments."

To discover the balance and to prevent burnout, we recommend knowing yourself first, and opening yourself to others so that isolation and exhaustion do not become dangerous enemies. Ways that we have discovered to prevent burnout in our own lives include planning for play, diversity in work, being accountable to a small group of friends and co-workers, and continuing to get help if we find ourselves in a "stuck" place.

In the next chapter we present a collage of independent-practice settings and professionals. Begin to design your own practice through the ideas and formats presented to you from others who already have done so.

2

CHAPTER

Portraits of Private-Practice Mental-Health Professionals

It was fun for us, and we hope helpful to you, to interview therapists who are currently in private practice. Through questionnaires and interviews we collected information on a variety of types of practices. In this chapter we highlight a few of them, with the idea that you will begin to creatively formulate your own practice. Elsewhere in the book we provide detail and concrete suggestions for practice building; here we offer you a time to dream and create a vision that appeals to you and your specialties.

Marcie Edmonds, MC, is a certified professional counselor who practices at Psychological Counseling Services in Scottsdale, Arizona. She has been in private practice for 6 years and is in a group practice with 14 therapists. Marcie specializes in treating eating disorders and is a licensed Focused Action Therapist. Marcie works with 28 to 30 patients per week and runs two groups. In addition to her clinical work, Marcie presents workshops on eating disorders, body image, and focused-action therapy. What Marcie likes most about private practice is the ability to do what she is most passionate about and not have to be a generalist. The environment in which she works allows her to be flexible and creative in her work. What she likes least about private practice is waiting for insurance reimbursements to come in, which makes it difficult at times to plan financially. Marcie's advice to therapists thinking about private practice is: "In order to be successful in private practice you must be able to create and implement a marketing plan. Take time to find your 'nitch' and identify your own style."

Carolyn Badila, LCSW, is a licensed clinical social worker who practices at The Therapy Center in Alexandria, Virginia. She has been in private practice for 12 years and is currently in a group practice with seven practitioners. The setting for her practice is a private outpatient clinic in which she sees, on an average, 25 to 30 patients per week. In addition to her clinical work, Carolyn is a supervisor and professional speaker. What Carolyn likes most about private practice is her patients; what she likes least are managed care, billing, and insurance issues. Carolyn recommends that a new therapist get some experience in a community mental-health center or inpatient setting in which he or she has the opportunity to see large numbers of varied patients and work with a variety of seasoned clinicians.

Marcus Earle, PhD, is a marriage and family psychologist who practices at Psychological Counseling Services, Scottsdale, Arizona. Marcus has been in private practice for 11 years and is currently in practice with 13 therapists. Marcus typically works with 35 clients per week and is cotherapist for three groups. In addition to his clinical work, he enjoys speaking and seminars. What Marcus likes most about private practice is the flexibility of time; least liked is the counterpart of time demands. His advice to someone fresh out of academic training is: "If you like to meet people and have them know you—then private practice is for you. It takes creativity, self initiative, and being an assertive person."

Lloyd Gillum, EdD, is a certified professional counselor who practices at Gillum and Associates in Phoenix, Arizona. He has been in private practice since 1991 and is currently in a solo practice. The setting for his practice is an office in Phoenix, in which he sees 20 patients per week. In addition to his clinical work, Lloyd, is involved in staff-development training and workshops. What Lloyd likes most about private practice is the sense of independence it brings; least liked are marketing, building the practice, and working with insurance companies. His advice to new therapists is: "Don't be afraid. You will learn more as you work in the field. Be a lifelong learner."

Ginnie Hartman, MA, LPCSW, is a private practitioner who works at The Healing Center in Spring Lake, Michigan. She has been in private practice for 15 years and is currently in a group practice of two therapists. Ginnie sees 20 individual clients per week and is involved in four groups. In addition to her clinical work, Ginnie does some professional speaking and teaching. What Ginnie likes most about private practice is her freedom from dealing with dysfunctional groups; least liked is the isolation from other colleagues. She advises other therapists to "get as much education as possible, and look for a specialty."

Diane Dillon, MA, is a private-practice counselor with Psychological Counseling Services in Scottsdale, Arizona. She has been in practice for 1 year and works with 13 other therapists and three interns. Diane has a caseload of 20 to 30 clients per week. Her professional activities include presentations, writing, and working as a teaching associate at Ottowa University. What Diane likes most about private practice is working with her clients and having a group of therapists with which to confer over tough cases. What Diane likes least is her struggle with her own boundary issues with regard to hours spent at work. Diane's advice to therapists thinking about private practice is: "Hook up with two or three other therapists—don't be a lone ranger."

Hermine Makman, MD, has been in private practice for 25 years. Hermine currently works from his home in solo practice. He sees a maximum of 30 patients per week. In addition to his clinical work, he has lectured and provided supervision for residents and interns. What Hermine likes most about private practice is "the chance to know people intimately: to hear their story and help with their pain; least liked is the sedentary life."

Doug Sorensen, LMSW-ACP, LCDC, is a social worker in Houston, Texas. He has been in private practice for 9 years and is currently in a solo practice. Doug sees between 35 and 45 clients individually per week and runs four men's groups. Doug does some professional speaking when he is not involved in clinical activities. What Doug likes most about private practice is "the freedom to be creative clinically and in an entrepreneurial sense—I love doing group work with men; least liked is the potential for isolation and some of the paperwork requirements." Doug advises new practitioners to have some experience before going into private practice. He does believe that there is room for private practitioners who know what they are doing.

Don Mathews is a marriage, family, and child therapist with a Master's degree in Clinical Psychology. He is the director and founder of the Impulse Treatment Center in Pleasant Hill, California. Don has been in private practice since 1981 and currently has a practice with three practitioners. Don sees 65 patients per week, and in addition he is a speaker and provides workshops for therapists on sex addiction. What Don likes most about private practice is the "freedom to be innovative, less cumbersome in new treatment styles, and more flexible hours; least liked is the influence of managed care and the constant need to get new clients." Don recommends learning a specialty that you are very interested in. It keeps your enthusiasm going as well as helping with managed care and gives others a way to identify you.

Brian Case is a marriage and family therapist at Psychological Counseling Services, in Scottsdale, Arizona. Brian is in a group practice with 13 other therapists and sees 20 to 25 patients per week. In addition to his clinical work, Brian serves on the faculty of two state universities. Brian enjoys the flexibility of being in private practice. He appreciates working with a cohesive group and helping people make significant improvements in their lives—and getting paid well for it. Brian likes least the up and down nature of income and lack of job security and benefits. His advice to others, "Go back! No really, to hold on to your dreams—don't sell out. You can make things work if you are determined."

Julie Wells, ACSW, is a credentialled substance-abuse and alcoholism counselor. She has been in private practice for 10 years and is in solo practice. Her private practice's name is Wellspring Therapy and Wellness Center located in Saratoga Springs, New York. Julie is involved in five groups per week and sees 20 to 25 individuals, families, or couples. Her practice is located in an old schoolhouse situated on two acres in a small city of 30,000 residents. When Julie is not working clinically, she speaks, writes a newsletter, and offers retreats and workshops. Julie likes most about private practice "the freedom to do the work I believe to be humane and effective and the ability to have flexibility in scheduling; least liked is the fear of financial insecurity, the managed care game, and problems with time management." Julie urges new practitioners to attend as many workshops or conferences in the field as they can and have interest in. Find a mentor in private practice—work part-time with him or her and part-time in an established agency.

Barbara Levinson, PhD, RN, CS, LMFT, works in solo practice at her Center for Healthy Sexuality. She has been in private practice for 7 years and sees approximately 85 patients per week. Barbara lectures and enjoys public speaking—T.V. news and radio. What Barbara likes most about private practice is her specialty of working with sex offenders and sex addicts. What she likes least is the isolation from other colleagues. Barbara recommends that you find a mentor in the community. Know what your conceptual framework is, but be open to all things. Have faith in yourself.

Belinda Wiens, MC, is a certified professional counselor who has been in private practice 1 year and in agency settings for 13 years. She is currently in solo practice and shares a suite of offices with two other therapists. Belinda sees between 18 and 22 patients per week on a part-time basis. When she worked in an agency setting, she would treat 35 to 40 patients per week. Her practice is located in Tempe, Arizona. What Belinda likes most about private practice is "setting my own schedule and reducing my hours; least liked is lack of contact with other colleagues and not being in the same building as psychiatrists and nurse practitioners—cuts out quick consultations."

Paul Hartman is a marriage and family therapist who has been in private practice for 6 years. He is in a group practice called The Healing Center, with three practitioners. Paul treats 30 individuals and 50 group patients per week. His practice is located in the small suburban town of

Spring Lake, Michigan. Paul likes most about private practice "the ability to put close to 100% energy into clinical work, setting my own schedule, and picking my own specialization; least liked is the lack of interaction with other professionals." Paul says, "Don't let managed care scare you. People need our services and will find a way to pay for them."

Peter Crockett is a licensed clinical social worker who has been in private practice for 13 years. He is in a group practice with seven practitioners located in Alexandria, Virginia. In addition to his clinical work seeing 40 patients per week, Peter is involved in training, supervision, and retreats. Peter likes most about private practice his "clients and group work; least liked is dealing with insurance carriers." Peter says, "Private practice is a wonderful experience. I came to the decision to work in this manner after a variety of important clinical experiences in the private sector. These earlier experiences helped me grow professionally and were invaluable."

As you can see, professionals in independent practice form a diverse group with similar characteristics. Although that may seem like a paradox, the truth is that the creativity in building a private practice is seemingly endless, and at the same time there are commonalties that weave themselves into the framework behind every practice. In the following chapters we explore those differences and provide you with the basic structure that is similar and oftentimes necessary for every practice.

Our goal is to provide you with the tools and ideas necessary for you to create your own professional profile, a private practice that suits your needs, experience, and professional goals. An independent practice is an evolving profile that changes with personal and professional growth as well as the needs of your community. We hope that you can see from our small sampling of a very large population that independent practice for mental-health professionals is alive and flourishing.

For a fun and sometimes insightful activity we encourage you to fill out the following questionnaire as your dream profile. If you are brand new to private practice or just beginning to think about becoming an independent practitioner, answer the questions as you think you might like your profile to look, at some time in the future. If you are a seasoned private practitioner, fill out the questionnaire as your ideal profile 5 to 10 years down the road.

This is the same questionnaire that we used in our survey of therapists who are in private practice and profiled in our book. Try not to censor your answers because of lack of training, financial constraints, or any other perceived limitation. Others have done this type of exercise through some sort of guided imagery by recording the questions on a tape recorder and using them through meditation to help create a visual image of their practices.

☐ **Private-Practice Questionnaire:**

Name:

Age (Pick an age you want to use for your visualization):

Professional title (license, certifications, specializations):

Group or solo practice:

Number of practitioners in practice:

Office staff (how many and job descriptions):

Patients seen per week: Individuals? Families? Couples? Groups?

Location of practice (location in state or country and type of setting):

Professional activities in addition to clinical work (e.g., speaking, writing, teaching . . .):

What you like most about private practice (guess if you are not currently in private practice):

What you like least about private practice (again, guess if you are not currently in private practice):

What advice would you offer to someone who is fresh out of academic training?

Another use for this questionnaire would be to give it to local therapists who are in private practice, especially if you are still in school or just starting your career. It is our experience that many professionals are willing to help others by sharing their own stories. You not only will get the opportunity to meet and network with other therapists in your area, but you will be able to see the diversity of practice in your locale.

PART

II

PUBLIC IDENTITY

It's a Matter of Marketing

Having a successful private practice truly is a matter of marketing. The word *marketing* strikes terror into many therapists. Graduate school and internships usually do not prepare a therapist for the unique world of marketing, yet an independent practice requires that marketing become a priority, an integral part of your career.

Many of us are afraid of becoming a marketing nightmare who approaches every person and event as a potential client or referral source. Sometimes we overcompensate and do no marketing at all. Marketing is a necessity of practice building, so what does appropriate marketing of a professional practice entail?

Ralph has an example in which a therapist in his practice came on a little too fast when he met with a physician. This physician liked to play handball and was a close personal friend of Ralph's. Ralph suggested that the therapist get together with the physician in order to get to know him and then have the possibility of referrals. The therapist, in his first meeting with the physician, suggested getting together to play handball. That was coming on too fast and basically pushed the physician away as opposed to encouraging him to come close and build a mutually satisfying professional relationship.

The opposite kind of example happened when a group of three attorneys were invited to speak to the group of therapists at PCS during a meeting of our staff. The attorneys asked the 13 therapists if anyone would be interested in doing a particular type of therapy and evaluation for them, and no one volunteered except for Ralph, whose caseload already was full. The reason given by a couple of therapists was that they needed to think about it. The problem is that the meeting was for only an hour, and it was important for those attorneys to know that the therapists would be interested, because there certainly were other therapists to whom they could refer. Times of opportunity do not come our way every day of the week and are certainly more advantageous than cold calls.

Another part of the above scenario is that sometimes as therapists, unless people are asking us to do exactly what we have already done a lot of, we become afraid of not having enough expertise. It is certainly important that we do not volunteer to do something outside our scope of practice; at the same time, from the points of view of both preventing burnout and building an independent practice, it may make sense to stay open to a number of options that can provide new frontiers for us in doing therapy.

The challenge in marketing independent practice is that the product is our own skills, and who we are in providing those skills. It has become painfully clear to us that someone may have phenomenal skills in business or in marketing other products and not be comfortable marketing his or her self—the product of doing therapy. Thus, it is essential that we examine ourselves and find out whether we believe that the product we have to offer in therapy is worthwhile and whether or not we are the right person.

We cannot state this often enough: If you want to be in independent practice, you must start thinking of yourself as a businessperson as well as a therapist. You are selling a service—therapy—and to attract customers (patients) you must market your service. Other professionals—physicians, veterinarians, optometrists—have had to face similar situations. As therapists, however, we often have faced our own and societal expectations contradictory to the notion of selling this service called therapy. We all have had at least one client say to us, "You're only doing this because you get paid for it."

If we stop, however, and are honest with ourselves, we have to admit that money is one way—certainly not the only way—we use to validate our therapeutic expertise, our education, and our training. For us to say to the mechanic who is repairing our car, "You're only doing this for the money," would be ludicrous. The mechanic would be highly unlikely to feel guilty; the "accusation" would be no accusation at all, merely a statement of part of the truth. Yes, the mechanic is doing the job for the money and because he or she is good at it, enjoys working with his or her hands, and feels a sense of satisfaction in the work.

We are no less entitled to payment for our services than is the dentist, the grocery-store owner, or the person who delivers our newspaper, all of whom do their jobs for the money as well as for less tangible reasons. In fact, calling yourself a businessperson in private practice is similar to being an employee of an agency: Both involve a contractual relationship that provides a service in return for pay.

Traditionally, business has distinguished between services and products (or goods). Services are intangible, usually centered on actions rather than material objects. You cannot store services nor take inventory of them. Services also are more dependent on people than on equipment or machinery. (These are broad distinctions. Think, for example, of the service implications of a restaurant's dishwashing equipment or an anesthesiologist's respirator breaking down.)

There also are differences between marketing a product and a service business. The distinction is not that the former must market its products but the latter simply waits for the customer to walk through the door; rather the difference lies in the marketing strategies that are most effective for a particular type of business. A general rule of thumb, for example, is that the more service-oriented the business is, the more marketing depends on word-of-mouth advertising and personal referral rather than on media advertising to be effective. There are some types of businesses that require little marketing. These are usually in new, "hot" areas with little competition. As soon as enough people enter the field, or the area itself becomes more commonplace to the general public, the days of the seller's market are over.

For instance, in 1971 when Ralph first started his practice, a therapist had the kind of service business in which you could hang out a shingle and wait for patients, and the wait would not be very long. Hanging onto this notion in the 21st century, however, ignores the reality that we are now in a buyer's market, and this kind of thinking almost certainly will result in failure of an independent practice.

Despite our stereotype of business being exclusively competitive, the history of American business is not just a tale of greedy robber barons driving others into bankruptcy and failure. Rather, American business also has a history of grass-roots networks of referral and mutual support. Many businesses began as small, family operations that grew because neighbors, shop owners, and the person who made deliveries used the service or product themselves and made referrals to others. Our marketing strategies all are based on a model of cooperation rather than competition. Cooperation is good business.

☐ The Implications of Cooperation

We firmly believe that in referrals "the more you give, the more you get." Too often, we worry about a limited supply of clients. In a way, such thinking undervalues our services and talents. To assume that few people use our services is to judge these services as not very important. Even if there were not a huge population from which to draw, we would probably devise methods and techniques to meet a variety of needs: We would find a way to adjust to the market. (To reassure yourself that there is a substantial market, simply take a look at the size of the self-help and psychology section in your local bookstore. Although "in" topics may change, the public's overall interest in psychological issues has remained consistently high.)

If all of us had completely full caseloads, if every in-patient facility and out-patient clinic were operating at capacity, and if new therapists continued to stream out of graduate school at the current rate, there still would be underserved populations.

Patrick Carnes is the clinical director for sexual disorder services at the Meadows in Wickenburg, Arizona. He is a noted author and speaker, and a personal friend of Ralph's. The ideal kind of relationship with a colleague is the kind of relationship that Pat and Ralph have, in which they regularly introduce patients to each other for continuing therapy, as opposed to being competitors in the field. This type of collegiality and cooperation is in the best interest of client care. The way Ralph and Pat support each other is by suggestions to patients that they read one or more of each other's books, referrals to workshops, and also referral to each other's services. Even though Ralph and Pat work in the same specialty area in the same state, they work together to provide help for clients that makes sense clinically and ends up making good business sense as well.

More important perhaps are the ethical implications of cooperation for our patients. It is inappropriate to assume that we can be equally effective for all patients. All of us have areas of particular competence—acknowledged or not—that best serve certain people. The same is true for our colleagues.

Consequently, a professional network among practitioners who refer patients based on each other's strengths results in the highest-quality care for the patient and a better reputation for our field—from which we all benefit. Most of us practice a particular type of therapy. When a potential client comes in, if we simply "fit" him or her into our program, we are doing that person and ourselves no favor.

Frequently the intake procedure is a good place to find whether or not there is a good fit for the therapist and the client from both points of view. We believe in "consumer protection"; thus, if someone else makes more sense either in the group at PCS or outside the practice, then it is our responsibility to suggest that the continuing therapy be with someone else. That also is true if the client believes that someone else makes more sense. The process then becomes to encourage that transition and, with written permission for a release of information, to provide data to whomever will be the ongoing therapist.

Ethically and practically, we think that developing appropriate cooperative support is a necessity. For example, we strongly urge therapists to have in place a system whereby they can reach a psychiatrist who will admit their client for evaluation within a few hours if needed. Everyone in independent practice needs that kind of backup; you get that aid by knowing your colleagues professionally and socially. You build that kind of backup by deliberately seeking it out.

It is also important to establish a network among several disciplines. At various times, you may need to be in touch with physicians, attorneys, judges, clergy, and so on. If a person came to see you in your role as therapist, but during the intake you noticed that the person's arm was bleeding profusely, to continue to treat the person as though he or she had only a psychological complaint would be unethical.

Most therapists are not trained nor competent to give legal, medical, or financial advice, yet these areas may be entwined in a client's treatment. It is essential that we are clear about our boundaries and have names available for referral if the client asks for them. Ideally it makes sense to give at least two or three names for possible referral.

If we are asked for a recommendation in an area in which we are not comfortable, in terms of our knowledge of the potential referral's expertise, then we tell the client that we do not have any names to give him or her. We never give referrals unless we have a working relationship with, or multiple recommendations from people we trust about a particular person. The advantage to being in an area for a length of time is that we have worked with attorneys and physicians and can give referrals in those areas.

Whether one is talking about cooperation between mental-health practitioners or between practitioners and other professionals, the focus is on developing a team approach—as appropriate—to a particular client's problem. Ralph cites the example of dealing with a mother and daughter who were seeing him for the first time together. The mother cited her daughter's eating disorder as a problem; the daughter denied that she had an eating disorder. Ralph responded by saying, "I don't know if you have an eating disorder or not. Your mother says you do. You say you don't. It's a tie vote, and I'm not going to vote until we have more information in order to make that decision. Since that is not an area I specialize in I would like you to see another therapist in our group, who does specialize in that area, for an evaluation. If she and you begin to agree that something needs to be done in that area, then I would like you to deal with her in that area."

Ralph also coleads groups with people who specialize in other areas.

This kind of team approach helps to ensure that the patient gets the most competent treatment available. At the same time, the therapist expands his or her referral base by involving and staying in contact with other professionals.

☐ Defining Success

A successful dynamic private practice is one that enables a person to maintain a lifestyle that best fits that particular person's needs, that is to say, that provides a balance that meets the person's emotional, physical, financial, and spiritual needs in a healthy way for that person. This can differ dramatically for one person or another.

It certainly is possible for a person to be unsuccessful in one type of setting and be extremely successful in another setting. For example, a therapist might not fit into the setting at PCS but fit well into some other practice that has different criteria.

If the first assumption underlying our marketing-strategy formulation is the need to base it on your own personality, then the second assumption underlying our marketing strategy formulation is the need to define success for yourself. Ideally your practice will be based not only on who you are but also on what you want. Endless techniques and instruments exist to assess your goals. You may find them valuable; however, what we are interested in right now is your personal, emotional definition of success.

The following questionnaire helps you clarify your definitions and priorities for personal and business success. You use the answers to this questionnaire in formulating a marketing plan (see Chapter 5).

☐ Success Questionnaire

1. Check any categories that apply and answer accompanying question(s).
   Success for me includes:
   Community service—What kind?

   Control of schedule—Defined as

   Education—What kind and level?

Freedom to take time off—How much per year?

Money—How much per year?

Number of patients—How many per year?

Power—Defined as

Prestige—Defined as

Publications—What kind? How many?

Referrals—How many per month?

Requests from colleagues for consultation—What kind? How many?

Time for family—How much?

Time for philanthropy—How much?

Requests for speaking engagements—From whom? How many?

Other

2. The three most important items from number 1 are:

3. The most important item from number 2 is:

4. To achieve Number 3, I would compromise:
Community service—What kind?

Control of schedule—Defined as

Education—What kind and level?

Freedom to take time off—How much per year?

Money—How much per year?

Number of patients—How many?

Power—Defined as

Prestige—Defined as

Publications—What kind? How many?

Referrals—How many per month?

Requests from colleagues for consultation—What kind? How many?

Time for family—How much?

Time for philanthropy—How much?

Requests for speaking engagements—From whom? How many?

Other

5. To achieve number 3, I would not compromise:
Community service—What kind?

Control of schedule—Defined

Education—What kind and level?

Freedom to take time off—How much per year?

Money—How much per year?

Number of patients—How many?

Power—Defined as

Prestige—Defined as

Publications—What kind? How many?

Referrals—How many per month?

Requests from colleagues for consultation—What kind? How many?

Time for family—How much?

Time for philanthropy—How much?

Requests for speaking engagements—From whom? How many?

Other

6. The most successful person I know is

7. I define that person as successful because

8. The person in numbers 6 and 7 is successful in business? Personally?

9. Success for me is more important:
   In business

   Personally

   Cannot separate the two.

   I am not really success-oriented.

10. Others see me as successful. Because

11. I define success as

12. I am/will be successful when/because I

13. When I am successful, it will mean that

14. To achieve success, I must
    Why?

    How?

    When?

15. I inhibit my success by

It is important to define success concretely. Often, when we have asked other therapists for their definitions, we have had to help them focus. It is also important to recognize that your definitions will include both tangible and intangible facets.

Listening In

Ralph (R): *Dorothy, being new to private practice what would your definition be for a successful independent practice?*

Dorothy (D): *My first thought is to be seeing as many patients as I want in the areas I want to specialize in.*

R: *How many patients do you want to see?*

D: *For me a full case load would be around 30 client hours. The rest of my week would be for writing, marketing, and staff meetings.*

R: *You mentioned areas you want to specialize in—what are those?*

D: *I'm not totally clear about that. I am trying out lots of things that interest me, and hoping to narrow my focus in the future. Currently I am in the process of being certified as a sex therapist, I am certified to administer assessments for engaged-married couples, and I know I want to pursue areas of spirituality and balance.*

R: *That sounds like you are already beginning to focus on certain areas. You don't have to move any faster than that. It is important to let your thinking evolve* *as you grow and experience different aspects of "doing therapy." Dorothy, what would you like for your practice to look like 5 years from now?*

D: *That's a great question and one I'll have to give some thought to. Initially I see myself working in three areas: counseling, writing, and speaking. I also have an interest in teaching.*

R: *What further training would you need to work in those areas?*

D: *I want to finish my certification process in sex therapy. I think I will probably continue my education to work toward a doctoral degree in psychology. Other than that I attend training seminars and workshops as they come up.*

R: *To support the lifestyle that you desire what does your annual income need to be?*

D: *I love to travel with my family and enjoy attending sports and theater events. We have three children who are either in college or will be attending college soon. Add that to regular household expenses, and I guess I need to make a lot. Actually, my husband has a good career and income so I see myself as wanting to contribute equally to our needs and wants.*

R: *What do you need to do to make sure you take care of yourself and family?*

D: *I can get out of balance quickly if I don't pay attention to my schedule. For me to be balanced I need to have time alone and with my family and friends on a regular basis. Alone time helps me stay centered and less anxious about all the things I have set myself up to accomplish. Family and friends let me know in a hurry when I am not paying attention to them.*

R: *Anything else you'd like to add to your definition of success?*

D: *Well, I have a question for you. How do you balance having enough patients to fill your schedule and having too many?*

R: *Figuring out and handling the juggling act of keeping a practice full is important in several ways to defining success—doing your practice building and having enough confidence to know there's going to be someone else; at other times, deciding how many patients to take. My own way of doing a practice is to "overbuild" it. I want to recommend that you think about it. I tend literally to overbuild always. If it's cut too close in an independent practice and something happens, your caseload can drop rapidly. We have had some people in our group who just built their practices to exactly where they wanted them, and then if something went wrong— the stock market went down, a facility closed down, a referral source dried up—it caused extreme anxiety.*

As you know I have set up our group to mitigate against sudden drop-offs. There are 13 people in our practice and interns, each of whom has a specialty area unique to himself or herself. As a group, we also try to have the advantages of both independent practice and a clinic. We're not a clinic, yet we work very closely as a team. We do family therapy but have these individual specialties that can be separately marketed—chemical dependency—addictions, hypnosis, groups for impaired profes-

sionals, vocational exploration, sex therapy, forensic psychology, supervision and training, intensives, couples communication, prepare-enrich, anger management, whatever it might be.

I tend to keep more people referred to me than I could possibly see myself, and I tell people in my group that I'll always be referring to the rest of them unless all of a sudden my caseload drops. If, when you start to define success for yourself in specific terms, you find that you don't want to worry too much about keeping a steady caseload, then you will have to devise strategies to protect against sudden drop-offs.

As you can see from this discussion, you may have to work to define the concrete particulars of success. The more concrete you can get, however, the more likely it is that your definitions will suggest strategies to help you realize success. For example, your definition of success may include the opportunity to work with interesting families and make a positive difference in their lives. Although this is an admirable aspiration, it does not give you any clues about how to realize it.

If, however, after further reflection, you recognize that you are especially fascinated by working with families in which chemical dependency is a major issue, and you have felt enormous satisfaction when you have worked successfully with this situation, then you have just identified a specific target market. Once you have a target market, specific ideas about how to reach that market begin to occur to you. At this point, you may want to go back to your success questionnaire and check to be sure that you have given the most concrete, specific answers that you possibly can.

☐ What Do You Have To Offer?

A third underlying assumption for the development of successful marketing strategies is a precise understanding of the product or service. In psychotherapy practice, the service is a hybrid of the therapist's personality, character, and experience; the theoretical or philosophical approach; and the techniques used that reflect this approach. What is unique about you and your approach? What are your particular areas of expertise? The answers to these questions provide the content for the marketing strategy. Who you are and what you do are what you are selling.

☐ Marketability Questionnaire

As you did with the success questionnaire, use your answers to the following questions to develop your marketing plan (see Chapter 5).

1. List three types of experiences that you have had that would be marketable (for example, worked with pregnant teenagers; have certificate in chemical dependency counseling; attended intensive continuing education seminar on child abuse):

2. List three skills that you think are the most marketable (for example, trained ability to read nonverbal communication; understanding of and ability to use systems theory in practice; ability to use Jungian sand tray):

3. List three services that you provide that are unique (or at least uncommon) in the marketplace (for example, do not charge for intake and termination sessions; do psychometric testing for own and others' clients; run a group for sex addicts):

The three questions in the marketability questionnaire are designed to help you distinguish yourself from other therapists in your locale by answering the question, "What do I have to offer potential clients that other therapists are not offering?" Once you define this clearly and concretely, as with the success questionnaire, you have a clearer idea of your market and how you can reach these people. If you have trouble answering the questions, you may want to think about what you would like to be able to offer potential clients and how to go about offering it. You may need to go back to school or attend particular continuing-education seminars. You may need to do an internship with a particular kind of practitioner or a particular facility. You may need to engage in activities different from your current ones. Do not just fantasize about what would be nice; develop a concrete strategy to realize it.

Let us move on to taking your private practice public.

Plurking Through the Network:
Taking a Private Practice Public

Plurking is playing while working and working while playing. When we are working seriously, there is still some enjoyment, a sense of playfulness, involved. At the same time, when we are playing, we still have some sense of our working selves. We both feel that learning how to plurk is a key to a successful private practice. The beauty of this concept is that it prevents the almost schizoid feeling that we are two people: the worker and the "real" person, or, as seen from a different angle, our old friends the entrepreneur and the helper. These two selves compete for time and attention, setting up a prime scenario for burnout. The plurker, on the other hand, is an integrated person capable of simultaneous productive concentration and enjoyment.

When presented with the concept of plurking, many people immediately think of the executive on the golf course, closing an important deal on the fifth tee. However, there is one requirement to defining this executive as a plurker: the person is plurking only if she or he enjoys playing golf! That is the difference between what we do, what we hope you will do, and what a "Hard Sell" does. A "Hard Sell" person forces himself or herself to endure any and every situation so that he or she can "work" it. That he or she only is doing something for the potential business is apparent to almost everyone; people absolutely doubt his or her sincerity and quickly lose respect for him or her.

What we are saying is, on the one hand, be aware of opportunities to play (enjoy, be challenged, be engaged, etc.) when you are working, and, on the other hand, be aware that opportunities for work (contacts, referrals, information sources) can and will arise when you are playing.

For us, plurking is a way of life. We have been asked if we have friends who are not referral sources. The answer is of course. At the same time, however, we realize that referrals come from unexpected sources and circumstances, so we keep alert to the possibilities. Plurking is a skill that you can apply when and where you choose. You can establish a comfortable "plurk level" consistent with the values and goals you have already established.

In thinking about how we can plurk in our lives, we find it most useful to ask, "What do I like to do that also may involve visibility for myself? The idea is to become involved in activities or with people in which you would get involved anyway, whether or not you were trying to build a practice.

☐ The Success Formula

Visibility is a key focus in the working-while-playing mode of plurking. Previously you defined for yourself the *what* of success—these goals, and the strategies to realize them, are different for each person reading this book. One principle, however, underlies whatever goals and strategies you choose: $S = V_e \times T$—success equals visibility sub exposure times time. Visibility means that you are *seen*; exposure means that you *reveal* yourself in order to educate others about what you do and are. Notice that we use the word "educate" rather than "sell"; marketing your business will be much less alien to you if you realize that you are involved in the process of educating individuals and the community about therapy itself, and not just about you. Visibility-exposure is related to time as a ratio: The more time you have been in private practice in a given geographic location within a given specialty area, the less work you have to do to be visible and exposed. Conversely, the less time for which you have been in private practice, or the less time for which you have been in a particular city or town or have specialized in an area, the more you have to engage in activities that give you visibility and exposure.

Ralph has been in practice in Phoenix since 1971. He no longer needs to spend 5 to 8 hours each week meeting, for example, with different organizations or giving various talks. Dorothy, on the other hand, is in her second year of private practice and definitely needs all the exposure she can get. One advantage she has as a new therapist is her longevity in the same community of over 20 years.

☐ Networking for Success

The many ways by which we gain visibility and exposure usually involve networking. Without question, networking has been the "in" business concept for a long time. *Networking*, a noun, has been twisted into a verb and parodied in the movies. Parody aside, networking is critical to marketing a professional practice. If we are uncomfortable with the idea of networking—everyone has some experience with its extremes, after all—we may conjure up the image of someone who flits from meeting to meeting, passing out business cards, and rarely finds time to actually practice.

This is not the model we endorse. Networking is simply the process of making contacts through formal organizations and informal structures, which allows you to get referrals and clients and to provide these to colleagues. Through sharing information, you grow professionally and contribute to the growth of the therapeutic profession itself.

Visibility is paramount to success in independent practice. What you do to make yourself known in the community is the process of networking. You interact with the community, and it refers people to you. You refer clients to members of the community; you support their businesses and organizations. Notice that interaction is bidirectional. In other words, you cannot simply give a speech (interaction in one direction) and disappear. You need to be available for feedback (referral, consultation, follow-up activities) from the community (interaction in the opposite direction.) Although you need to be active in the community to receive referrals, the referrals themselves result from your accumulated activity rather than any particular activity.

Of course, not every activity is equally useful from a networking standpoint. We both have discovered that by being involved in certain activities, not as therapists but as people who enjoy certain shared activities with particular groups, we keep running into the same groups of people. If you are networking with a large enough group of people regularly, you increase your chances that these people will think about you when someone they know needs a therapist.

Ralph enjoys jogging, but he has not built his practice around the activity even though he sometimes meets other people while jogging. This does not mean that he must give up jogging because it does not build his practice; it does mean that he recognizes that his reasons for jogging have little to do with his practice, and he does not pretend that he is building his practice when he is jogging. On the other hand, Ralph also plays golf. He belongs a club whose membership includes the kinds of people his group practice tends to attract. We do not believe that people are going to be able to judge our therapeutic skills by meeting us on the boards of the symphony or the theater or in a sports league; they will, however, get a feel for us as people.

Dorothy's other career choice is writing. She splits her time and energies between counseling and writing. For her, writing involves attendance at national conferences, meeting with other writers, and contact with editors and publishers. Those are natural times of plurking with others who are not necessarily exposed to the therapeutic community. When she is actually in the process of writing, she is not involved with anyone or anything other than her computer. Those are not marketing times by any stretch of the imagination, at least until the writing becomes published.

Ralph often quotes Virginia Satir who, when Ralph was in graduate school, responded in a letter to his inquiry about what makes a family therapist? *"The person qua person is more important than the methodology."* This is the bottom line whether we are talking about what makes a good therapist or what makes an effective marketing strategy.

Positive and Negative Visibility

There are many different ways to be visible; anything that makes you visible contains some possibilities for networking although, as we have pointed out, some activities are better than others. Do not overlook the givens of your life at a particular time. Anytime you interact, you are perceived. We like to summarize this idea as, "wherever you go, there you are." Whether you are in your bathrobe running out in the rain to grab the morning paper, or arguing with a sales clerk over his or her tediously slow handling of your purchases, there you are. Whether you want to be there or not.

Frequently, when we talk about plurking, some therapists say, "I don't want to do that, that's not for me. I want to work from 8 to 4 or 5, then I want to go home, go hiking, or sit with my family. I don't want to be aware always that I'm looking for clients." We are not trying to say that you should not have separate time for yourself. For most of us, some separate time is necessary. We also are not saying that you should run your whole life around what is best for business. We would become dangerously close to automatons if all our decisions were based only on business. What we are trying to say, however, is that even if you do not want to be aware of potential clients, you must be aware that potential clients are looking at *you*.

For example, when you go hiking, and someone hikes by you, but you pretend not to see them because you are on your "off time" and do not want to be invaded or bothered, what kind of message are you sending to that person? What reaction does the person have to your message? What image of yourself are you leaving with that person?

Appropriate Behavior

Bad news travels faster than good news. If you are in private practice, bad news about *you* can wipe you out quickly, and bad news about others in the field affects all of us. It is important that we keep our own noses clean and help each other do the same. We need to recognize what the average citizens of our communities—assuming for the moment that these people are our target market—regard as acceptable behavior.

You may choose to step outside the acceptable context of a given community, but if you do, you need to understand and accept both the effects that this has on people's (read: potential clients') perception of the therapeutic community and the limits it imposes on your ability to market your own practice.

What we really are talking about here is the concept of *appropriateness*. There are many levels of appropriateness that apply to greater and lesser degrees. For example, the ethics codes of various professional organizations describe one form of appropriateness that applies across the board to all the members of the organization (and that nonmembers with similar kinds of training and practice should think seriously about emulating, even if they decide not to belong to the organization.)

Norms for appropriate dress, on the other hand, are usually specific to a given geographic area. For example, Ralph used to live in Boston, where the dress tends to be more formal than in Scottsdale, Arizona. The dress that would tend to make people comfortable in Scottsdale would probably have the opposite effect in Boston, and vice-versa.

Appropriate dress also is determined by such factors as the type of client your practice currently serves, the ambiance of your office, and your target market. You probably are going to experience a credibility problem if you show up at IBM in sandals; conversely, you may put off a group of teenaged dropouts if you show up for a presentation in extremely expensive or overly formal clothes. (Beware, however, that you will probably experience the same problem if you try to dress like the teenagers themselves!)

Again, we are not trying to make good and bad judgments—at least about dress; ethics is another matter. What we are saying is to always be aware of the impact that going outside the norms of appropriateness has on your practice, and to plan your marketing strategies accordingly. If you feel very strongly, for example, about dressing a certain way, you may want to locate your practice (geographically or in terms of target market) where your way of dressing is appropriate.

Targeting Your Networking

To market your business successfully, you need to analyze your market. One of the ways to do this is to target your networking. Networking is not just activity done for the sake of being in motion; it involves conscious decisions about the most efficient ways to get information you need, to let key organizational decision makers know what you do, or to make individuals who have need of your specialization aware of your existence.

Some people confuse joining organizations—any organization will do, they think—with networking. If you join an organization and are not active, the result may be worse than if you had not joined at all. At the same time we do not mean to imply you should limit yourself to individuals or groups with which you have something in common. For instance, you probably have a lot in common with members of a professional association of therapists in your specialty area. Joining such an organization can be very important to your professional growth—one goal of networking. But the pool of referrals available from this group, a second networking goal, probably is fairly limited, because you all practice the same specialty. Therefore, another kind of group may better serve your second goal.

Increasingly, networking is occurring not only between individuals but also between groups. At PCS we have therapists who colead groups together, pooling their individual clients and referrals, in order to create an atmosphere conducive to the type of group being offered. Another type of group networking occurs if a number of solo practitioners form an informal network in a defined locale.

Whatever arrangement you participate in, it is our opinion that networking among groups is becoming almost essential for those who want to bid on contracts with small- and medium-sized corporations. Two groups getting together to cobid contracts can create a much more attractive package for a company, because they can offer a range of services and specialties.

Additionally, cobidding can make capitation contracts (that is, charging a set rate per employee, an arrangement that is fast replacing the fee-for-service contract) much more feasible. Because capitation contracts depend on obtaining a large number of clients to be profitable, two groups working together would be much more likely to handle this client load.

You may need to check the requirements of a corporation's particular insurance company before embarking on a group bid. Usually, you can create a joint-venture agreement between two group practices to contract with the corporation. If the insurance company requires a single employer contract with the corporation, a joint-venture agreement probably will not work.

Refer Unto Others: The Two-Directional Flow

As we have mentioned, networking needs a two-directional flow in order to work. Thus, networking is not exploitation; it is instead an exercise in mutuality. We provide referrals to colleagues and, in exchange, receive referrals from them. For us, the process comes down to this: The more you give, the more you get. The process starts as a dyad and ends as a myriad. An exchange between two colleagues can ripple out in numerous directions.

It is important—from both ethical and business standpoints—to support those who support you. Even so-called competitors have more to gain from sharing information, services, and referrals than they have to lose. After all, various professional groups such as psychiatrists and psychologists have attained legitimacy (read: status, financial remuneration, access) with group action that created a group identity in the public's eyes.

If you are competitive, you are focused on your competition and not on yourself nor your business; that is, you are reactive, making decisions in light of what your competitor does, and not proactive, doing what is best for yourself and your business. You also need to use common sense. Make sure you believe in the other's product, whatever it is. If you do not use or refer to someone who is giving you referrals, the considerate thing to do, if confronted, is to let the person know why as politely as possible.

Although obviously this often is difficult to ascertain up front, you should try to get a feel for a person's character, competency, ethics, and so on before you cultivate a referral relationship. Try to do your homework about another person's area of expertise, training, and experience. In other words, take the referral process seriously. Refer to whom you know and be known to those referring to you. Networking is not a substitute for professional competency.

The referral process can be intricate and take time to develop. Many professionals make the mistake of expecting instant rewards in the form of referrals for their networking efforts. If you speak before a Rotary Club or a church or temple and say, "Gee, it's been 3 weeks since I spoke and no one's come to see me," you are letting your feelings get "hooked into" in a way similar to what can happen in therapy itself. You can create a very oppressive situation for yourself that is unrealistic.

You may not hear from anyone, or five people may walk in the next day after you do a presentation. Someone who heard you speak 3 years ago may suddenly call and make an appointment. There is not a one-to-one correspondence between a single activity and number of referrals; rather you must focus on your overall activity and results.

Ralph once did a talk show in Phoenix on sexual addiction; the phones hardly stopped ringing. He was told that the response was highly unusual. That day, he just happened to hit on a topic on many people's minds—a matter of coincidental timing. Ralph also had a person walk into his office who had heard him speak 15 years before. The client needed help and found out Ralph was alive, functioning, and still in Phoenix, so she sought him out.

The quirkiness of the referral process underscores the need to establish positive name recognition. Yes, the more ways in which you can get your name in front of the public the better, but you had better make sure your name is associated with positive recognition. Otherwise you could find yourself being remembered 15 years later not for an impressive lecture but as the person who embarrassed the whole audience by making a joke offensive to the elderly.

Putting Your Referrals to Work: Record Keeping and Follow-up

To get the most from the referral process, keep records and follow up with your referral sources. Record keeping is the raw data from which you can learn about the market you are attracting by monitoring who is sending you referrals, who your most active referral sources are, and what kind of person is being referred to you. To aid this process, we suggest you keep a list of referrals, including the name of the person, when the person called, who referred the person, to whom the person spoke, whom the person saw the first time, and to whom the person was finally referred (if applicable).

This list is useful for a variety of activities and analyses. For example, you can invite the people on the list to an open house or send them announcements of new groups you are forming, new specialty areas, new associates, and so on. You also can use them as contacts for various organizations of which they are members and of course keep the list as a record for your follow-up responsibilities. You can analyze who is sending you what kind of referrals and how frequently.

This may sound like a cumbersome job, but it does not have to be.

There are many fine computer programs designed to track that type of information and organize it in such a way that the information is easily accessible. For those of you who are not fully computerized, there is a simple way of tracking information by using 3 × 5 cards and indexing them alphabetically in a card holder. One easy way to acknowledge referral sources on a consistent basis is to note their birthdays and send cards or small gifts. A birthday is more personalized; your gift does not get lost in the sea of gifts during holidays; and the cost for you is spread out throughout the year.

The Importance of Follow-up

Follow-up with referral sources is more than politeness, it is essential to the process, especially if you hope to obtain future referrals. The referring person is interested in the results of his or her actions. In addition, referral follow-up is an opportunity to thank the person for the referral and to keep your name in the referral source's mind. Sometimes, the client's treatment depends on a team approach and ongoing communication between, for example, the primary physician, an attorney, and the therapist. Too often, this team approach is overlooked.

In Ralph's group, with the client's or the family's written permission to waive confidentiality, the therapist communicates with the referral source and others who are going to continue to be involved in the family's life (for example, physicians, attorneys, judges, clergy.) As a sex therapist, Ralph often sees people for a specific problem within some larger treatment context. Ralph will send a letter marked "confidential" with a cover page stating, "Dear [referral source], Thank you for referring [client's name]. I have this person's written permission to communicate with you. If there is anything additional you would like me to know, please contact me and I'll do the same with you." Inside the cover letter, there is another smaller envelope stamped "privileged information, only to be opened by [referral source, physician, attorney, etc.]." In this envelope is a letter Ralph has dictated (again, with the client's written consent) detailing how he sees the situation and stating his desire to work as a team with the person.

This strategy is important to developing that sense of connectedness discussed previously and part of the ongoing process of working with referral sources. Ralph has received feedback over the years from many of his referral sources explaining that they refer people to him because, in addition to being a competent therapist, he lets the referral sources know that they are appreciated and he keeps them apprised of the referred client's status and situation.

How to Follow Up and Stay in Touch with Referral Sources

What kind of follow-up you do is an individual choice based on your personality. Some people invite their referral sources to lunch periodically or to open houses. As mentioned, we often write follow-up letters; other therapists are more comfortable on the telephone, although phone contact depends on the people involved. If you are calling someone who is not going to return your calls, then you are not covering yourself in terms of responsibility.

Another way to stay in touch with referral sources is a termination follow-up letter. The therapist can write a letter (with a release-of-information form that is current from the client or family) to the referral source saying, "So-and-so is not coming in to see us anymore. Here are some of the things that happened. I appreciate the referral, and if I can be part of a team in the future, please don't hesitate to call, etc." Another thing to keep in mind is to seek written permission from the new client to thank a referring client. Some clients might not want the referring client to know that they are seeing a therapist, so obtaining written permission protects you against a charge of violation of confidentiality.

Occasionally, you will discover—again, by analyzing regularly your referral list—that referrals from a particular source that were once abundant have begun to drop off. It is best simply to contact the person and try to find out why. Be straightforward, for example, saying something like "I noticed that 2 years ago you gave me "x" referrals, and last year it was "y," and this year it's even less. Is there something going on that I should be aware of?" In some cases, the decision has nothing to do with you: It could be that the facility at which the referral source works has contracted with a specific group for mental-health services, or the source has changed direction or position and has fewer occasions to refer. The problem could be miscommunication between a referral source and your support personnel. You need to make it clear to referral sources that you welcome feedback from them regularly, and you need to work to maintain clear communication among you, your referral sources, and the support staff or colleagues with whom you work.

Giving Back to the Community

If you are an active networker with a large number of referrals coming in and going out, sooner or later you will have to deal with the issue of pro bono work, specifically how much and what kind you want to do. You will be asked to do gratis work: seeing people with no insurance, giving assistance to social-service agencies, giving presentations or seminars or writing articles for networking organizations to which you belong—the possibilities are endless.

There are no rules governing your level of participation in these activities. You may choose to fulfill certain kinds of requests because you believe in their inherent value; in deciding about other requests you will want to weigh the visibility and exposure you get against the time and effort required. You may want to keep in mind that the more serious you are about making sure that your clients who can afford to pay you actually *do* pay, the freer you are to engage in pro bono work for clients who cannot pay.

Stylistic Subtleties

In addition to basic common-sense practices in networking that we have mentioned—acting ethically, being honest about what you can and cannot do, knowing those who refer to you and to whom you refer—are some we might call "stylistic subtleties" having to do with the psychology of networking.

Ralph created the following role-play conversation with one of his workshop participants. Although it may seem an obvious example of what not to do, we have both had experiences with people who have done what Ralph is dramatizing. "Ralph" is discussing his need for referrals with a "doctor" with whom "Ralph" has worked a couple of times in the past, and "Ralph" is trying to persuade the doctor to refer to him:

Ralph (R): *Say, Bill, how are you doing?*

Participant (P): *Quite well, thank you.*

R: *I want to share something. You know that I do marital and family therapy and I'm really hurting right now, just don't seem to have any patients. Since we've worked together in the past, I'd like you to know my situation and can you help me out?*

P: *How far are you from our emergency room? Well, I'd be glad to keep you in mind. Why don't you give your name, address, and phone number to my secretary?*

R: *Okay. You know I've been going through a lot of problems in my marriage, my wife has kicked me out and the divorce will cost me a lot of money. I've stayed pretty busy but I need to get busier right now. I know you're a caring person and I really need referrals right now.*

P: *Do you need some time to talk?*

R: *Well Bill, I'd like to talk, but right now I'm so busy trying to build my practice and stay ahead of all my financial needs, but please remember I do need to have more clients, okay?*

P: *I'll do that.*

After this dialogue, the participant pointed out to Ralph and the rest of the workshop participants that he probably would not have sent clients to "Ralph" based on this interaction alone. Rather, whether or not he referred would be based on the nature of his ongoing relationship with "Ralph." The prospects for "Ralph" would be uncertain at best.

Actually, we never could see ourselves speaking this way. Not because "Ralph" was not telling the truth, but because it is the opposite of the attitude and behavior it takes to build a practice. Coming from such an overt position of need as "Ralph" does in this dialogue is probably going to make people very uncomfortable and immediately ready to question your professional ability, at least at this point in your life. It is similar to telling a new client at an initial session that you are really glad to see him or her because you need him or her or financially you are hurting or you have gone through something like he or she is going through.

It is important in the networking process to maintain a positive image of yourself as a successful person in demand. We are not trying to say that you should lie or fake your way through a contact saying, "Oh, I've got a successful practice and I can't see you for several weeks," when in fact you have nothing on the calendar. But neither is it useful, for example, to say to a client setting up her or his first appointment, "When would you like to come in? I can see you anytime this week, anytime of day, 8, 9, 10, 11 . . . " Too often the person responds with, "I'll call you back later." Instead, say, "Would you like to see me Tuesday at 10 or Wednesday at 3?" This way you are responsive to the client's needs without sending "rescue me" messages.

To be successful in independent practice, it is important to have a sense of realistic power, being in charge, and confidence that you will succeed. With clients, and occasionally referral sources, you do not want to appear more nervous than they are, or you risk making them more anxious than they already are.

Recently Dorothy attended a seminar to be certified to administer a marriage assessment for engaged couples as well as those who are already married. During the seminar she sat next to a pastor who also was attending the seminar. At a break she introduced herself, and they discussed their roles when working with couples. The pastor made a comment that the church he worked for was in the process of turning over their counseling needs to local agencies; they would be interviewing prospective therapists in the next few months.

Dorothy followed up that conversation with a phone call asking for an interview and an opportunity to be considered as one of the referral sources. The pastor remembered her from their brief exchange at the seminar and encouraged Dorothy to send information and meet with him. She did not come on too strong during the brief time they spoke at the conference, and she followed up immediately when she learned of the opportunity opening up at this large church.

This approach works for several reasons. First, Dorothy respected the limited time she had in which to interact with the pastor at the seminar. She heard of an opportunity and made a mental note to follow up with a phone call. She gave the pastor the opportunity to see a sampling of the resources available through the agency at PCS by premailing brochures to the pastor for review. She reinforced her interest by establishing specific dates and follow-up.

In the 21st century therapists will have to be increasingly creative in devising ways to interact with people who can provide referrals. Many therapists have pointed out to us that cold calling seldom works anymore. Solo practitioners who work in large cities especially sometimes find that even if they work hard to keep themselves visible through follow-up letters and phone calls, they are forgotten 2 or 3 months later in the large pool of therapists. You have to find other ways to get to know people and let them know you as a person. One way is to offer yourself as a speaker to personnel conventions and addictions conventions.

☐ Getting the Word Out: Additional Ways to Network

We have pointed out general principles of marketing and mentioned a few suggestions for networking; we now would like to offer additional ideas for ways to increase your visibility.

Advertising

The issue of advertising and its effectiveness frequently comes up when we talk to therapists. We have mixed feelings about, and have had mixed results from, formal advertising. When other therapists are asked to cite strategies that did not work as marketing tools, many people mention direct mail, one form of print advertising.

It has been a general maxim in marketing that the more intangible your product, the more personal contact and personal recognition is required to sell the product. Conversely, a tangible, concrete product benefits most from advertising. Although as a general guideline this principle is probably true, specific situations can contradict it.

Certainly, we find the professional announcement useful in terms of creating name recognition. We sometimes send an announcement when someone is new to our group with the person's name and specialty. The announcement creates name recognition for the new person, and for those of us in the group already known in the community, the announcement is a reminder of our presence. Obviously, moving your practice would be another situation in which you would want to send an announcement, also reminding people about your specialty areas. Another kind of announcement that we find useful is the specialty list, which names each of the people in the group and their particular specialty; one can add a brief explanation of each area.

The notion of specialty announcements relates to another form of advertising: Yellow Pages listings. Ralph has found that the most specific of his listings, Sex Therapists, has brought the most referrals, perhaps because, of all the categories under which he is listed, in metropolitan Phoenix that category has the fewest number of practitioners. It is sometimes helpful to list under a professional association, such as the American Association for Marriage and Family Therapy, if one is included and you are a member. Such a listing implies a level of expertise and credentials not apparent in more general listings.

You might say, "In a whole year, I only got three or four clients from that listing." Those few clients pay the cost of the advertisement, and it is quite likely that they may do more than that in terms of networking and referrals. It is important that potential clients be able to find you in the Yellow Pages after they have obtained your name elsewhere and are considering seeing you.

Radio, Television, Newspaper Columns, and Books

Expertise and the ability to communicate information about specialty areas in the mental health field are vital for radio and television appearances or newspaper ads. Ralph has found it useful to get to know the programming directors of radio and television stations when he has been interviewed for programs. Ralph then sends his group's specialty list to the programming director. When something happens in the community, which is what the director keys into, he or she starts looking around for somebody who can talk about, for example, child custody, or mediation, or domestic violence. Ralph has made himself useful enough in the past to programming directors so that now he has several directors who automatically call and say, "Ralph, I need a person who can talk about this." If Ralph knows someone with expertise in the area, and can help the director do her or his job, he eventually sees the result in his practice.

Writing an article or a column for a newspaper, a local magazine, or a newsletter or writing a book is another effective networking technique.

Obviously, the more regularly you can write for a publication, the more name recognition and credibility you develop with the reader. Although writing an article here and there or writing a letter to the editor in and of itself may not be enough to bring someone in, these more sporadic activities can trigger name recognition if the person has heard of you or known of you in other contexts.

Dorothy has written articles for the Phoenix newspaper that have been published, and she writes a continuing series of small thoughts and devotionals for a national publication. We both continue to write books for professional and nonprofessional audiences, which provide name recognition as well as speaking opportunities. Obviously, a book with widespread distribution provides opportunities for networking on a national level.

Specialty areas are not for everyone and are not easily duplicated. We mention them to help you get your creative juices flowing and to widen your ideas about networking. Think about your passions and interests and see how they might complement your work as a therapist.

Community Visibility

We have mentioned community service and educational activities: serving on boards, doing other kinds of volunteer work, and giving lectures, workshops, demonstrations, and seminars. These activities can be directly related to your work (lectures on your specialty, donated therapy sessions, etc.) or they can run far afield. You may think that general volunteer work is less valuable to practice building than is an activity directly about your work, but this is not the case. As you give others assistance through the theater, the symphony, the crisis shelter, or Little League, people see that you are available, they see you in public, walking and talking, they see that you do not have horns, and they say, "Ah, I can refer to that person," or, "That person may know where I can get some help." In other words, you convey the impression of trustworthiness as a person, and this impression includes the professional aspect of your life.

Of course, you also could look for volunteer activities that relate directly to your work. Many civic and charitable organizations constantly are looking for speakers to address their regular meetings. Look for organizations whose charitable interests relate in some way to your area of expertise. For example, if you have expertise in domestic violence you might speak before a group of women or men and staff from a local shelter. If you have expertise in addictions counseling, you might speak before a Lions Club meeting that focuses on drug awareness programs.

Cross-Marketing

Networking may lead you to possibilities for cross-marketing with either another therapist or a related professional whose practice somehow dovetails with yours. Cross-marketing is the practice of combining resources with another person or institution for marketing, with the goal of generating more business as a result of the association.

Open Houses

Another networking technique that we have found effective is the open house or breakfast. Again, if you expect a lot of people to begin automatically coming to your office or referring to you just because you have an open house, you are probably going to be disappointed; it just does not work that way.

The open house should reflect your image. In other words, do not expect to get many referrals if your fee schedule says "high class" but your open house—your promotion, the food you serve, the decor, the atmosphere—says "shabby" or "cheap." Clashing images can produce backlash instead of growth. Bottles of pop and chips and dip from the grocery store, unless you are at the lower end of the overhead and fee spectrum, will not do. When we have open houses, we make sure that we are conveying an image consistent with our practice as a whole: We have the event catered; we send printed invitations; our dress and the office's decor are neat, clean, and appropriate.

Ralph sometimes "piggybacks" two networking events: His group will hold an open house from 4 to 7 in the evening for which the mailing is large in order to foster name recognition, even among those who do not attend the event itself. Sometimes 350 people will attend. After the open house, a select group of about 40 people from the open house are invited to go out to dinner at a good restaurant. These people are often those who have been particularly good sources of referrals in the past or who may be expected to be good sources in the future.

Some people have been skeptical of the effectiveness of this two-part event, citing the expense of both an open house and dinner, but, as with other networking techniques, if you receive four or five referrals who subsequently become patients, you have paid for your open house and dinner and gotten an enormous amount of "free" visibility.

When you have an open house, you do not just invite neighbors, you invite people who have been good to you professionally to thank them. (Use your referral lists!) Also, target people whom you want to know—invite attorneys or physicians located near you. Not only do you create opportunities for yourself, you also help these people make contact with each other. In their subsequent dealings with each other, your name may come up yet again. Even if they do not attend, you have begun to create name recognition. Calling the people you have invited a week or two in advance to tell them you are looking forward to seeing them also can help boost attendance.

A few cautionary words—be cognizant of your scheduling. It is sometimes more effective to schedule an open house or party or breakfast during an unusual season. Everyone has Christmas parties. People get sick of them, and you probably will not get as much mileage from them as you would from a Valentine's Day party or Halloween party.

Plurking is really at the heart of the idea of independent practice as a lifestyle rather than as a job, a career, or even a vocation. We hope that, after reading this chapter, you can see that the plurking style you develop should be as personal as your therapeutic style. Have fun with marketing—let your ideas and style flow as you grow and change throughout your career.

CHAPTER 5

Mapping Your Success:
Marketing Plans and Specialties

Professionals are in the position of being able to market themselves more as experts and consultants, and less like individuals with something concrete to sell. Hopefully Chapter 4 has convinced you that marketing is survival for the private-practice business. In this chapter, we address the components of a marketing plan and examine how they work. In addition, we discuss the marketing aspects of specialization—the why and the how to—using an example from Ralph's experience of specializing in sports psychology.

☐ The Marketing Plan

Marketing involves a process that begins with an analysis of your needs and the market's needs, moves toward goal setting based on current and future projections; and results in a plan for implementation. In other chapters we look at personal traits and an individual's uniqueness in the marketplace. You can integrate this data with basic marketing principles to develop a marketing strategy specifically designed for you.

Your personality determines the style of your marketing strategies; your marketable qualities and the service of therapy supply the content of the marketing plan. The information that you generate about your definitions of success determines the limits of your business and, in turn, the type and amount of marketing you need to do. All of this information underpins the marketing plan.

Technically, the marketing plan is a document derived from the process of planning your marketing strategy. Although the document serves as a guideline, it is the planning that is essential. For this reason, you might choose to hire a marketing-research consultant to draw up the plan, although we think you will be remiss if you are not actively involved in the planning process. The plan itself is composed of four sections: needs assessment (both your needs as well as the current market needs), short- and long-term goal setting, action strategies, and ongoing evaluation.

Needs Assessment

This section relates to earlier discussions of your personal and professional goals in relation to the market. That is, what do you want and how do the number of potential clients, the competition, and your access to the potential clients match up? The needs assessment includes statements about:

1. Your goals
    a. The answers to your needs assessment in Chapter 1
    b. The answers to the success questionnaire in Chapter 3
2. Analysis of your services (refer to the marketability questionnaire in Chapter 3)
    a. What are your credentials and experience?
    b. Do you have a particular area of expertise?
    c. Are you in solo or group practice?
    d. What is your therapeutic conceptual base (Adlerian, systemic, integrative, psychodynamic, behavioral, etc.)?
    e. What are your professional affiliations?
3. Target clients
    a. Who are your potential clients (families, individuals, corporate executives, etc.)? Be as specific as possible.
    b. What type of therapy do you want to offer (group, individual, or both)?
    c. How many clients constitute a full caseload?
4. Demographics of your area
    a. How many potential clients for your targeted group live in the area where you practice?
    b. Do you have access to clients who live in other states or even other countries?
    c. Will you be in one location or several?

5. Competition, direct and indirect
    a. How many therapists with the same or similar credentials are practicing in your geographical area?
    b. How many therapists of any type are practicing in your geographical area?
    c. How many competing clinics or hospitals are there in your area?
6. Market attitudes in your community
    a. What is the public attitude in your locale toward therapy and therapists?
    b. What is the general reputation of therapists?
    c. What is the public attitude toward your specialty?
    d. How generally known are you in the community?

Case Example

As a case example we outline a marketing plan for Jill, a therapist who is just beginning to build a private practice. We also examine her marketing objectives and marketing strategies in each of the next two sections.

Jill began her career as a Master-of-Counseling intern at a private practice in the Midwest. Her goal after internship was to continue working in private practice with a group of professionals. She began formulating a marketing plan to reach her goals of working clinically, marketing, and speaking during her internship.

Analysis of Services.   Jill, in addition to her degree goals, was certified to administer premarital assessments and train parents through parenting courses. During the last phase of her internship, she began the process of working toward certification as a sex therapist. Her areas of interest included addiction work, spirituality, sexuality, and family systems. The theoretical base she most identified with was Adlerian, although she had attended workshops in gestalt, Jungian, and behavioral methods to allow her to customize her approach to the client's needs.

Memberships she held during her first years of practice included being a member of the American Counseling Association, the American Association of Sex Educators, Counselors, and Therapists, and several community organizations.

Target Clients.   During her first year of practice, Jill was still in the process of identifying her target clients as she discovered what types of clients were the best fits for her. She liked working with couples, individuals, intensives (full-time outpatient therapy), and groups. She had not worked with very many teens or children at that time. The areas she wanted to target were relationship issues, spiritual issues, sexuality, and addiction work.

Demographics.   Jill found it was not unusual to have clients travel from all over the greater metropolitan area in which she worked for treatment at an agency or therapist of their choice. Her area may be somewhat unique in that people are used to traveling across town, or even the state, to accommodate their needs.

Competition.   Jill's competition included over 500 listings in the Yellow Pages under the heading "Counselors—Marriage, Family, Child & Individual." That listing included agencies, which meant that there were probably groups of counselors included under single umbrellas. In addition, there were several other listings for counselors or therapists under different headings.

Market Attitudes.   The public attitude toward therapy was, and is, generally supportive, as evidenced by the large number of treatment facilities in Jill's area. Local mental-health organizations offered monthly educational programs focusing on different aspects of therapy, and radio and television often featured professionals to comment on their current topic. Most of Jill's clients came from speaking in the community, personal referrals, or the agency where she was employed.

Goal Setting

Marketing goals are time-based, observable intentions. They reflect the situational analysis in that they refer to your goals and present your attainable ambitions, given the market demographics, attitudes, competition, and accessibility. Effective marketing goals are stated precisely and with measurable outcomes. Typically, marketing goals consider the following:

1. Size of the practice
   a. What is the maximum caseload desired?
   b. What is the target date for achievement of goal (e.g., "The practice will serve 25 clients by September 25")?
2. Specific indication of services, current and projected
   a. Exactly what services do you now offer?
   b. Are there new services that you wish to offer?
   c. What is the target date for new services (e.g., "In addition to the

current caseload of 10 individuals per week, I will see five families and conduct two groups by May 4")?

Case Example: Jill's Marketing Objectives

Jill wanted to fill the time she devoted to therapy and focus on people with relationship, spiritual, and lifestyle issues as her target group for her services. Thus, Jill's goal was to lead or colead two groups per week and have a caseload of 20 to 30 clients per week. She planned to achieve her goal within 6 months to a year after finalizing her marketing plan.

Action Strategies

Given your situation, that is, the work you do in your particular community, strategies are the specific formulations that you devise to meet your objectives. Many therapists consider this part of the marketing process to be the most creative and enjoyable. The specifics of networking and referral generation discussed in Chapter 4 provide ideas for developing your action strategies. Look for activities that let colleagues and the public know that you exist as a competent and caring practitioner.

In considering the strategies, the wise marketer analyzes his or her current and past practices, looking for what has worked in the past and what has not. Before you develop the third part of your marketing plan, you may want to consider the strategies that have been successful (meaning that they generated clients or contacts who subsequently referred clients to you) and those that did not seem to work very well. The "follow-up" category in the following analysis is included to nudge you to speculate on a way to rework or retry the strategy for more success. Keep these in mind when you work on your new marketing strategies: past strategy, outcome, and follow-up.

Preparing action strategies requires that you answer the questions posed in the needs-assessment and goal-setting sections. An efficient way to conceptualize strategies is to list the objectives that you developed and then brainstorm some possible techniques to realize each objective.

Case Example: Jill's Action Strategies

In order to meet her goal of filling her practice, Jill needed to become more recognized in the community and let those who did know her know the type of work she did. Jill had a marketing background in sales and utilized some of that knowledge in her current career. She also knew her strengths as well as her weaknesses in marketing.

Jill's action strategies included:

1. Calling on one pastor or church per month to meet and discuss the services offered at her agency as well as personal specialties
2. Cofacilitating a marriage-preparation seminar once a quarter
3. Sending an announcement of professional services to people and companies with whom there is an ongoing relationship
4. Making a list of small companies and medical practices in which a key administrative person or owner was known to her personally, within 1 month
5. Making appointments with the people from the list in number 4, at minimum one per month
6. Having a professional brochure made that could be used to market her speaking topics as well as her counseling specialties

Ongoing Evaluation

It is important to emphasize that your marketing plan is fluid and will change as you grow and expand in your practice. There are certain times when change naturally needs to occur such as personal and family changes, health changes, relocation, moving toward retirement, establishing new credentials or skills, and market shifts.

We suggest that you review your plan on a regular basis, whether once a quarter or once a year. Document the changes that you make in your marketing plan so that you have a road map to follow and a journal to look back on. In addition to regular reviews, situations inevitably will arise that force you to reevaluate your plan. We suggest that you look at changes as opportunities instead of failures. It is sometimes easy to get "locked into the plan" instead of letting the plan be your guide. Remember that there are no failures unless you quit trying.

Discussion

If you look back at Jill's complete marketing plan, you can see how each section proceeds logically from the previous section. The marketing plan, then, is the record of your data collection about your goals, the feasibility of meeting those goals in the market in which you are located, and the means by which to achieve those goals.

In preparing a marketing plan you do not have to rely exclusively on your own creativity. There are a number of ways to learn about research-marketing techniques for small businesses and professional corporations.

In addition to consulting marketing books or hiring a marketing-research specialist in your community, you might discuss techniques used by your successful colleagues or plan a marketing forum with local experts for one of your professional-association meetings. Most communities of at least moderate size offer "entrepreneurial training" programs for the small businessperson. Economic development corporations, which often are branches of local government, are becoming more interested in helping small businesspeople. The federal Small Business Administration also conducts seminars in marketing and offers excellent materials on marketing topics, and under its auspices the Service Corps of Retired Executives offers free, individual consulting to small businesspeople.

☐ Areas of Specialization

In our opinion, the decision to specialize has many advantages. The most obvious is that one usually chooses to specialize in areas in which one has expertise, that are enjoyable, and that produce the most positive results—in other words, areas in which the chances for therapeutic success are high. Specializing also can help you tailor your work schedule and environment.

From a business perspective, the increasing competition demands a more targeted market. Specialization can focus your marketing effort and create a niche—that is, an area of practice in which a very specific need exists in your market, which you can fill. Once established within this niche, you are likely to get more referrals from a greater variety of sources. The burgeoning field of chemical-dependency counseling is a perfect example. From alcohol counseling came a model for other drug-dependency counseling; from other drug-dependency counseling came a model for codependency counseling. Clearly, the trend in contractual arrangements between independent practitioners and hospitals or healthcare plans decidedly favors specialization.

Following is a very partial and personal list of specialties that we think are in demand now and show signs of remaining that way in the 21st century. Based on your own experience and that of your colleagues, you probably are able to think of other specialties not listed here:

Adult children of alcoholics
AIDS counseling
Career counseling
Chemical dependency
Child sexual-abuse therapy
Child sexual-assault prevention
Codependency

Corporate counseling
Counseling children of divorce
Counseling for the elderly
Counseling gifted children
Counseling infertile couples
Displaced worker–relocation counseling
Domestic violence
"Down-sizing"
Eating disorders
Employee-relations counseling
Exit interviews
Expressive-arts therapy
Grief counseling
Organizational development
Parenting skills
Sex-offender treatment
Sex therapy
Sexual-addictions counseling
Spirituality
Sports psychology

Once you have decided to specialize, you need to assess your skills, training, preferences, and the types of clients in your practice. You also need to examine the needs of your community. If this process sounds familiar, it is—it repeats basic marketing planning found earlier.

Determine if your specialization requires additional training, certification, or licensing. Several options are available for training: university and continuing-education classes, reading materials, internships, workshops and seminars, certification programs, cofacilitation and supervision, and affiliation with professional organizations, hospitals, and mental-health delivery systems.

If your specialization encompasses a need that has been identified recently, your opportunities for training in traditional settings likely are limited, and you will be best served by ferreting out those individuals already working in the area and reading as widely as possible in related areas. Although training may be more difficult to come by, you will be in a good position to market a specialty on the cutting edge of therapeutic practice.

A cautionary word about specialization: The therapist has a dual responsibility. On the one hand, the therapist should become familiar with a wide range of therapeutic modalities and topics, including those covered in the mass media. On the other hand, the therapist is required to represent his or her qualifications and knowledge accurately and without embellishment. Reading a couple of books does not constitute a specialization. You owe it to yourself and to your clients to take advantage of every opportunity to develop your specialty: reading, consultation, internships, continuing-education classes, and so on.

Case Study—Developing a Specialty: Sports Psychology

One of Ralph's specialty areas is sports psychology, which addresses issues specific to being an athlete. These issues may include performance anxiety, the role of competition, and family stresses resulting from name recognition, travel, off-season and in-season changes, contract negotiation, and mood fluctuations. Ralph offers such services as life planning to help an athlete develop an identity outside sports, seminars for those in particular sports that deal with issues specific to that sport, and direct clinical services for families and individuals.

Ralph began focusing on sports psychology in the early years of his practice. A well-known sports figure, Reggie Jackson, and Gary Walker, his agent, both of whom he knew personally, asked him to provide help for some teammates. Under the auspices of the United Development Company, Jackson and Walker were offering a program called "Life Planning" for athletes, and they asked Ralph to assist them. Ralph realized that even though sports is a big industry, and that being able to handle moods, feelings, and problems is very important to an athlete's performance, the mental-health field, at that time, for the most part had ignored the area. Ralph also realized that he personally enjoyed sports and interacting with athletes, and his group practice already contained some therapists who specialized in areas, such as biofeedback and hypnosis, relevant to the practice of sports psychology.

The Phoenix area, in which Ralph practices, is a sports center of sorts: A number of professional athletes make their homes there, and the city is the home of professional baseball, basketball, hockey, and football teams, and host to professional golf and tennis tournaments. Ralph contacted some coaches, whom he already knew from other contexts, to find out what they thought was needed and talked to athletes themselves to assess what services would be most beneficial to them. He noticed many similarities between professional athletes and the high-profile corporate and professional people with whom he had extensive experience. From this information, he devised programs and techniques to meet the needs he had identified.

Ralph developed a 3-hour seminar on identity issues, stressing the idea that an athlete is a person first who also happens to be an athlete. He put together a group for athletes that examined the challenges involved in dealing with the mood swings associated with performance or its lack. He met with individuals and groups of athletes to help them deal with issues they faced as they finished college, went through the signing process, and became professionals.

Choosing to specialize in sports psychology, in addition to providing personally satisfying work, also helped Ralph build his practice and a national network. At the time, so few people were specializing in the area, and so Ralph enjoyed little competition and very high visibility.

Ralph points out that learning about sports psychology has become more systematized as literature and training programs—including seminars, internships, and supervision—have become available. To break into the field now, he suggests getting to know colleagues who specialize in this area and meeting with athletic directors and coaches. Forming associations with high schools may provide valuable experience in the field before trying to practice at the college and professional levels.

Specialties can be formulated at any stage of your career. For someone just starting out it is important to understand that the process of establishing yourself as a specialist can be frustratingly slow and difficult. We suggest that a good place to start is while you are in school or working on your internship. Reading widely in professional journals and topical books and searching oneself in order to discover interests is a good first step. Although it is useful to be aware of areas of great demand and popular interest, in the end your personal interest and excitement about a particular specialty are the best guides to choosing one.

If you are in midstream, you may discover that you are facing marketing challenges that dictate the success of your specialty. It might make sense for you to expand into different specialty areas or move toward a completely new area. The evolution of a practice involves a constant dialogue between therapeutic and business interests and often results in changes in a therapist's area of specialization. One of the biggest mistakes made by therapists is trying harder to do the same thing. What they do not typically do is to try something innovative, creative, or different.

Developing an area of specialization requires the same creativity and innovation necessary to build and maintain an independent practice in general. It is not something that you do once and then forget. Even if you stay in the same general field throughout your career, in order to keep your practice flourishing and yourself fully engaged you must remain open to the revolutionary possibilities that present themselves.

6
CHAPTER

Institutional Affiliation

You now have some good ideas about how to take your private practice public, thus creating an independent practice. You may begin to wonder, however, about maintaining your independence in the face of burgeoning megainstitutions, which provide an ever-increasing percentage of healthcare services in this country. Although these are not all large organizations, the trend is toward consolidation.

At times there are advantages to affiliating with institutions. Perhaps the most obvious advantage is that marketing and building a practice usually are easier if one has access to the large clientele that these institutions represent. Hospitals often serve as referral hubs in an area, both through direct referral of their outpatient clients and through referral from staff clinicians who become part of one's professional network.

Cross-marketing with an institution provides referrals and name recognition; in other words, you become the beneficiary of the marketing, advertising, and public relations efforts of the institution. For example, a community hospital advertises in the local paper that a well-known therapist will give a workshop and sell copies of her most recent book. The hospital and the therapist have shared the cost of advertising, and both benefit from the connection. Hospitals also are in a good position to provide you with an overview of clinical and marketing trends in mental-health care. Other advantages include educational opportunities through in-service seminars, access to team therapy and concomitant clinical feedback. The decision then is not so much whether or not to affiliate, but how.

Nevertheless, many independent practitioners fear that affiliation will result in the loss of the autonomy that they sought in the first place by becoming independent practitioners. These fears sometimes are supported by reality.

Affiliations should be mutually beneficial. The institution receives the benefit of your knowledge of the needs and attitudes of your community, your professional expertise, and the marketing of your reputation without having to provide you with employee benefits. Too often, however, private practitioners forget the value that they bring to the institution. They tend to approach the institution in an obsequious manner because they diminish their own professional value and potential contribution.

Moving from contact to contract involves three major steps: market planning (once again), negotiation and contract, and implementation. Two thirds of this process, you will notice, revolve around business skills rather than therapeutic skills, with good reason. Dealing with highly structured corporations requires access to either your own or an advisor's business expertise. In this context, business naivete can seriously compromise your practice.

☐ Marketing Planning

To create an effective affiliation, the first step is to assess the marketplace. This time the market consists of any type of institution that has the possibility of referring mental-health clients for therapy: mental-health facilities (hospitals, clinics, etc.), medical facilities (physicians, dentists, hospice organizations, etc.), religious institutions, and corporate institutions. Another affiliation that is beneficial includes the mental-health components of healthcare organizations. In this chapter we will deal with institutional affiliation, and in the next, managed care. When you were doing your marketing plan, you probably included an analysis of the institutional market. Because your analysis was not specifically focused on institutions alone, you may have some gaps in your information.

☐ Negotiation and Contract

As in any business transaction—from setting a client's fee to closing a contract with a major institution—negotiation is inevitable. The most appropriate stance in these negotiations is win-win, that is, a negotiation in which the interests of both parties are integrated into the final outcome. However, assume that the burden of responsibility for a win-win interaction rests with you. This does not preclude fair-mindedness by the institution.

Win-win negotiations require you to employ many of your therapeutic skills, but to a different purpose. The intended outcome is a contract that is mutually beneficial for the client, the institution, and your practice. You need to listen actively, evaluate the communication process, respect yourself as well as those with whom you are negotiating, be clear, and be honest.

☐ Implementation

Implementation is a two-step process. The first is the obvious carrying out of the services for which you have been contracted. The second process actually consists of analyzing and positioning yourself to receive additional contract opportunities, that is, repeating the market analysis and negotiation process. As you become more familiar with the institution, you are in a better position to know the gaps in its services and the areas in which it intends to develop. Once inside the workings of the institution, you can suggest areas in which you can fill its needs and become an active participant in strategic planning. Of all the steps involved in affiliation, implementation is the most individualized.

☐ Institutional Connections

The best way to explain how institutional affiliation can benefit your practice is to give some examples from professionals who have been involved in them. As you read the following, let your imagination begin to develop inroads into your specific marketplace. Creativity and determination play a dominant role in expanding your practice through these means.

Hospital Affiliation

Identify the hospitals in your area in which you have some sort of personal connection with staff members. These people need not be in administration, although they should have connections with administrative staff. Obtain permission to attend staff meetings. This is a good way to meet other professionals, often results in gaining their support, and can lead to referrals.

If you do not know anyone who can help, attend some of their local workshops. Many hospitals put on regularly scheduled seminars and workshops for the public. These are a good way to see what they already are offering and what might be a need you can meet, and certainly a good way to meet the people who are presenting them and working with the hospital. One of the objectives is to build a relationship with the chief executive officer and other persons who can help you get in the door professionally.

Ralph worked with Samaritan Behavioral Health Center (formerly Scottsdale Camelback Hospital) for several years. He had a personal relationship with the chief executive going in, and he developed programs that were mutually beneficial for him and the hospital. During that time he ran a program for sex offenders at the hospital. The hospital provided space for him to work and promoted his services through speaking engagements and book sales. Ralph led two groups a week, participated in staffings, and provided training for staff. The hospital invited attorneys and other therapists to be part of the training and speaking sessions.

Prisons

Marilyn Murray, a therapist at PCS, spent a great deal of time doing pro bono work at the Arizona State Prison in Florence, Arizona. Marilyn is author of *Prisoner of Another War* (PageMill Press), a book that deals with her own recovery from victimization as a child in which she was gang raped in Kansas on her way home from school. During her work at the prison, Marilyn established a close working relationship with the former director of the Department of Corrections, Sam Lewis. Her work helped her to gain national recognition as an expert therapist in treatment of sex offenders. Marilyn was the right person, given her own victimization, to deal with this population. This is an example of pro bono work with an institution that led to professional specialization and contacts that benefited Marilyn's own practice and the clients she works with.

Insurance Companies

Another example of a unique opportunity for institutional affiliation is Ralph's participation with an insurance company that had approximately 1800 employees. Ralph's role was to see employees and their families who needed counseling. Supervisors of the company or the employees themselves could refer for therapy. PCS's name and phone number were posted throughout the insurance offices. Meetings were held on a regular basis in which Ralph spoke to all of the employees about mental-health concerns and services.

The financial agreement stated that the company would pay the entire cost of the intake session and then 75% of the cost of other sessions up to

12 to 16 sessions per year. If more sessions were needed, they would be requested and reviewed by the company psychiatrist.

Some of the seminars in the workplace were on smoking cessation, stress management, communication skills, and lifestyles. The company paid 100% of the cost of providing the seminars, including Ralph's fees.

Ralph held this contract for 6 years and then the insurance company changed their medical/mental-health contract. It is important not to have any one affiliation as your only source of income. Contracts change all the time and sometimes with very little notice.

Religious Institutions

In our area some churches, temples, and other religious organizations have their own counseling centers. More frequently we find that the mental-health needs of the people who attend religious services are referred outside the religious center. Sometimes a pastor or clergy member will see the individual or family once and refer to an appropriate therapist.

There are many ways to connect with religious institutions such as co-sponsoring seminars, providing divorce-recovery workshops, offering pre-marital counseling seminars on campus, and many others. It is easiest to get in the door if the religious institution matches your own belief system. If you want to expand beyond that, it is important for you to be open to whatever belief system the institution holds and to communicate your acceptance of their beliefs during negotiation and initial meetings.

Marcus Earle and Dorothy provide marriage-preparation seminars through local churches. These are 1-day workshops designed to meet the needs of engaged couples or recently married couples. Marcus works with the couples on communication skills and family-of-origin issues during the first half of the day. Dorothy administers a marriage assessment to the couples prior to the seminar and then reviews the inventory during the second half of the day. In some churches in our location weddings are conducted every weekend of the year. It can be a very lucrative and fun way to interact with potential clients.

Utility Companies

Another unusual affiliation Ralph held for 10 years was with a major utility company in the area in which Ralph worked. There were several aspects of service rendered, and the PCS staff of therapists often was involved. One of the areas of service was to administer tests to prospective employees as part of the interview process. Four to five PCS therapists would periodically go on-site to do evaluations for potential employees.

Another service was to meet with the administration staff and board to teach communication skills. The therapists that dealt with that area attended actual board meetings to help utilize the skills they had learned during the meetings. It is wonderful to have a contract that lasts such a long time. Remember, during that time be thinking about and working on other marketing contacts so as not to depend on the current one always being there.

Physician Groups

There are numerous ways to be involved with a group of physicians. Ralph began his practice in an obstetrics and gynecology group in Scottsdale, Arizona. In 1971 he joined the group as a psychologist in practice with three physicians. This not only helped build Ralph's practice through referrals but also introduced Ralph to the medical community in his area. Ralph continues to have a good working relationship with physicians throughout the greater Phoenix area.

Currently PCS has a contract with the Board of Medical Examiners to monitor their impaired-physicians program. In addition to offering individual sessions with a therapist at PCS, Ralph runs a weekly group for impaired physicians.

Attorneys

Attorneys use professional therapists as witnesses in court cases for many different reasons. Among them are child-custody cases and sex offenses. If you are interested in working in the court system, you can market yourself to large or medium-sized groups of attorneys as a possibility for institutional affiliation.

You also could offer your services to the group of attorneys as a therapist and in-house consultant. Certainly there is a great deal of stress that is unique to attorneys, and they may welcome seminars on stress management and communication skills, to name a few.

Some therapists are taking their practices on the road by meeting with clients in their own office settings. For professionals, such as attorneys, who are "schedule overloaded" your offer of being on location each week might be very marketable. Confidentiality issues would have to be addressed up front and structured according to the setting you are in.

☐ **Exercise for Creativity**

We have given you a brief look at some of the ways in which institutional affiliation has made sense and worked profitably for a few therapists. This exercise is designed to get your juices flowing and help you identify areas in which you might begin to expand through affiliation.

Fill in the following chart by first listing institutions that are located in your practice area. Create broad headings such as hospitals, and then break them down into subheadings with specific names such as "Memorial Hospital" and so forth. Next, go back and list names of people you know in any capacity who are employed by those institutions. Finally, choose three to five institutions that interest you and with which you want to pursue an alliance. Keep the list handy in case the first ones you choose do not pan out. Add to the list as you think of new names and places. We have created a sample heading with subheadings to get you started. Try to have at least 5 to 10 headings complete with subheadings and names before you finish.

1. Hospitals
   a. Lincoln Hospital
      1. John Cameron— hospital CEO
      2. Claire Evans—surgical nurse
   b. Memorial Hospital
   c. St. Joseph's Hospital
   d. Community Care Hospital
      1. Mary Davies—Chief of Staff
      2. Bob Turner—ICU nurse

CHAPTER 7

Managed Care:
Mystery or Mastery

Many practitioners have had some experience affiliating, usually with hospitals, clinics, or social-service agencies. Based on our experience, and that of many of our colleagues, we believe that health-maintenance organizations, employee-assistance plans, and preferred-provider organizations, as well as variations on these three structures, form an increasingly lucrative market.

Because mental-health care delivery has become so diverse, understanding the variety of structures, and how to operate effectively within them, allows the independent practitioner more flexibility in tailoring a practice. The downside of this diversity and growth, however, is the volatility of the industry. The consensus of those who monitor healthcare-delivery trends is that the movement toward alternative delivery and financing of healthcare is permanent, but the structures remain in flux. Consequently, our suggestions for evaluating your potential relationship with these structures are offered as broad guidelines for you to adapt to the situation in your community.

The change in delivery of services is based on the key concept of managed mental-health care. This concept can be understood in two ways: Financially, it refers to a strategy of predetermining cost limitations for services; clinically, it refers to an approach to therapy emphasizing brief outpatient care. All of the alternative delivery systems that we discuss are variations of this basic concept. Each system has its own focus, but none is inherently superior to the others.

☐ Definition of Terms

Capitation: A method of payment in which the provider is paid a fixed fee for each patient served regardless of the number or nature of services provided. Profit increases as the amount of services is reduced.

Carve-out programs: These programs separate the managed mental-health/substance-abuse care program from the rest of the medical plan. They often are requested by employers in an effort to better track increased mental-health spending.

Case management: This addresses both price and utilization. Managed-care operators use case managers to provide ongoing management of treatment plans.

Continuous quality improvement: An industry-proven method for balancing cost with quality, now increasingly being adopted in managed care.

Copayment: Out-of-pocket cost to the consumer.

Employee-assistance program (EAP): Program designed to deal with problems in the workplace that may diminish productivity; may be internal or external.

Exclusive-provider organization: A hybrid between a preferred-provider organization and a health-maintenance organization created by self-insured companies for their employees; restrictions similar to health-maintenance organizations.

Exclusion: Medical condition or type of treatment not covered by a plan. Some plans exclude mental-health treatment.

Gatekeeper: A healthcare professional, often a primary-care physician, employed by a managed-care entity to authorize access to specialty care by beneficiaries or enrollees.

Health-maintenance organization (HMO): Provides prepaid services to members with minimal copayment. Some are structured on a wellness model. Members usually must use plan facilities and providers.

Indemnity plan: Another name for major medical insurance.

IPA (Variously interpreted as *independent provider association, independent physician association,* and *individual practice associations*): Like HMOs, lower-cost, prepaid health plans with fixed charge for members and limits for number of therapy sessions. Unlike HMOs, members go to provider's office; also can refer to an organization of providers formed to negotiate contracts with HMOs, preferred-provider organizations, hospitals, and so on.

Managed health care: The control of healthcare utilization, quality, and claims using a variety of cost-containment methods. The expressed goal is to deliver cost-effective healthcare without sacrificing quality or access.

Preferred provider organization (PPO): Group of providers with whom employers, insurance companies, or other third-party payers contract; paid on a fee-for-service basis at a lower rate than the usual fee.

Self-insurance: A health plan in which the risk for medical cost is assumed by the employing company rather than an insurance company or managed-care plan. Self-funded plans are exempt from certain requirements applied to other health plans.

To function effectively in the managed-care setting, in which a premium is placed on short-term care, many therapists need retraining or additional training. Learning to speak the language of managed care is a starting point. Our "miniglossary" is a place to begin to familiarize yourself with terms that may or may not be known to you at this point in your career. In addition, some therapists need additional training in doing short-term work, assessments, diagnosis, and solid evaluations.

In general, managed care seeks to reduce outpatient therapy expenses by controlling access through the following steps: preauthorization for services; utilization of review, which frequently limits the average number of visits per episode of care; and preferred-provider panels, which require clients to see only certain providers who have agreed to use a brief therapy approach and to accept the discounted fee.

Preauthorization for services is important to note because as a therapist you may need to think through some of the ethics of the managed-care environment. Confidentiality issues such as making sure you release *only* information necessary for review or precertification processes are relevant to the patient's specific treatment needs.

Patients need to be informed about how the precertification and utilization-review processes work. Sometimes patients are shocked to learn that the authorization is for only three to six sessions. Other times they are disillusioned to find that they are not "cured" in the time specified, thinking that they are not progressing as rapidly as they should.

There are areas of managed care that may present concerns or difficulties to the independent practitioner. Identifying aspects of managed care that may be concerns, and learning to deal with them effectively, will help you in your practice and with client care. Potential areas of concern include possible restricted consumer access to practitioners who are not medical doctors, inadequate quality and levels of mental-health services, unreasonable cost containment, and possible client abandonment. One way to manage the concerns and difficulties is to read and be knowledgeable about current trends and their impact on the therapeutic process.

The issue of client abandonment might involve premature termination of treatment because of the denial of authorization to provide further care. This is an important issue and sometimes tough to sort through. As a therapist, you may have to challenge the denial through formal appeals of the reviewer's decision. At other times it may make sense for the therapist to offer pro bono sessions, take reduced fees, or make the referral to an appropriate individual or agency so that the treatment may continue uninterrupted.

With all of these concerns we, as therapists, need to know the answers to certain questions each time we evaluate working with a managed-care company. Those questions include but are not limited to:

> What type and how much treatment may be authorized?
> What services are covered?
> Who makes the utilization review and authorization decisions?
> What are the utilization-review criteria and how may they be appealed?
> What are the expectations for access to treatment, information, and clinical records?
> Who has access to confidential information and how is it safeguarded?
> What restrictions may exist for referring to other providers for outpatient or inpatient care?
> What financial incentives are present for those who make referrals and authorize treatment sessions?

Moving from managed-care considerations, let us look at the different forms of managed care that currently exist. There are varieties and types within each form, and our list is not an exhaustive one. We present the major care systems that you will more than likely encounter as a mental-health therapist.

☐ Health-Maintenance Organizations

HMOs are healthcare plans that deliver comprehensive, coordinated medical services to voluntarily enrolled members on a prepaid basis. HMOs as independent companies hire their own staff and establish facilities to provide a variety of healthcare services to their members at costs below those of traditional delivery systems. Membership costs are based on a flat rate per member and are prepaid, usually by an employer. Patients pay a small membership fee per paycheck and a flat copayment at the time of service. The HMO covers services provided by its staff in its facilities; it also may cover, at least in part, emergency services sought by members traveling outside the service area.

HMOs were devised according to a preventive wellness approach to healthcare service and cost containment of medical care based on a treatment philosophy of limited intervention. Most HMOs limit the number of therapy sessions they cover. The emphasis for treatment is on brief therapy.

For the independent practitioner seeking part-time agency employment, the HMO may be of help and provide you with many opportunities. If you are just beginning to build a practice, working for an HMO may allow you to make connections and build a network in your community. An HMO offers little opportunity to those who solely want to practice independently, unless they affiliate with a PPO or an IPA, that in turn contracts with an HMO.

☐ Individual Practice Associations

An IPA is a type of HMO that makes contractual arrangements with providers who have incorporated to deliver services on a fee-for-service or capitated basis. Capitation is a reimbursement system in which service providers are paid to provide services for a large population of individuals. Rather than being paid on a fee-for-service basis, the contractor is paid to provide all the healthcare services for that population on a per-member, per-month basis. The contractor is paid the same amount of money, whether the population uses a large amount of services or a small amount of services.

Joining an IPA might be a serious consideration for the private practitioner, both because it is a way to counter the large organizations that threaten to overrun private practice, and because it is an ideal marketing opportunity for referrals. Before signing, look at who or what determines the organization's standards of care, composition of peer-review committees, specialty representation, assurances of patient confidentiality, and grievance and disciplinary procedures.

☐ Preferred Provider Organizations

Almost all PPOs refer patients directly to lists of participating therapists. PPOs differ from HMOs in that PPOs can contract providers from a variety of sources—for example, individual practitioners, group practices, or hospitals. These providers are independent contractors, not employees as in an HMO arrangement. In a PPO, providers are paid on a fee-for-service basis; in an HMO, providers are salaried regardless of services provided, although the members who are most productive may be rewarded with higher salaries or bonuses. The purchaser of PPO services pays a monthly fee; the client also may pay a small monthly fee, and the client also pays a copayment at the time of service. The PPO does not own the service facility. If a client needs to be referred to a specialist, both PPOs and HMOs generally expect the referral to be to a practitioner within the service organization.

Exclusive provider organizations differ from PPOs by having "lock-in" arrangements, meaning that clients are required to use their services. This is opposed to the usual PPO practice in which clients have incentives, such as lower deductibles, to use providers on the PPO's list but retain the option to use other therapists. Therapists are organizing or joining PPOs as a way to preserve at least some of their autonomy. Healthcare mergers are taking place, at a rapid rate, to create conglomerates that threaten to devour the independent practitioner.

The general criteria for selecting providers include state licensing or certification and practicing within the right geographic area. Practitioners must agree to go along with all the specific requirements of the plan: preadmission procedures, utilization reviews, and the rest. Therapists who join PPOs agree to accept the fee schedule established by the organization. Therapists who were trained in many different orientations have an easier time getting on the lists.

☐ Employee-Assistance Programs

EAPs are company-based programs to identify and treat problems affecting job performance. An EAP program can be internal or external. Internal programs, usually limited to very large companies, hire their own clinicians; external programs refer clients to outside clinicians. Clinicians, although not necessarily members of the same group practice, are designated by the company as a PPO.

The choice to become a vendor should emerge after a practitioner has cultivated relationships with respected colleagues and corporate decision makers. Typically, a vendor is an independent contractor who provides assessment, referral, and case-management services for the company, as well as brief therapy. Those clients who require longer-term therapy are referred. At the point of referral to a longer-term primary therapist, payment is assumed by the company's insurance.

We offer some tips for therapists seeking to affiliate with an EAP provider: First, we recommend that you develop a specialty relationship with the EAP. Offer to furnish services other than counseling (workshops, seminars, and testing). Be willing to work nontraditional hours that meet the needs of the employees. Contact the director of an existing EAP and visit his or her office. Network with other professionals in your area to ask them about their EAP experiences.

Some of the ways in which a private practitioner can work with EAPs include being on the referral list of national programs that use local clinicians for some services, getting regular referrals from the companies in your area, and setting up and managing your own EAP service.

EAP pay scales tend to be higher than other managed-care contracts; thus, competition for EAP-related work is increasing. Graduate programs are more aggressively pursuing placement in EAPs for their graduates and interns. Workplace knowledge is critical to be effective in your pursuit of EAP contracts. The therapist needs to know about corporate culture and how mental health can benefit the workplace.

☐ Marketing Your Practice in Managed Care

There are several ways to market yourself to managed care systems. Some of the ways you can put yourself in the best position to be considered include the following:

1. Do an inventory of your clients to have information about the types of services and treatment you routinely offer.
2. Learn the specialized jargon of managed-care systems. We have provided you with a list of the most commonly used terms to date. Continue to expand your lexicon through reading and seminars on managed care.
3. If you notice that you have worked with several clients from the same local employer, then you have a possibility of expanding your clientele through that resource.
4. Be prepared to be flexible on your rates, which can mean anywhere from a 10% to 30% discount on your current fee schedule.
5. Consider joining a group of independent practitioners if you are in solo practice. A group is more marketable than a therapist who is on her or his own. If you are considering a group, look for one with a wide range of specialists.
6. Read the managed-care contracts carefully. That statement leads us to the next phase of the process: understanding the differences in contracts and organizations.

☐ Contracts and Companies

Learning to read a plan's proposed contract critically and understanding the key terms of the contract are becoming essential skills for the protection of a therapist's livelihood. In our opinion some contracts simply are not worth signing. Contrary to popular myths, managed-care organization's (MCO's) contracts are not merely carbon copies of each other. They can vary significantly. Here are a few questions to keep in mind when reviewing contracts.

1. Who are the parties involved? Recognizing who the contracting parties are helps identify issues such as whose rules govern, how the therapist is paid and by whom, who can change the rules, when the therapist can terminate participation, and who else can terminate the therapist's participation.
2. What kind of MCO is it? Knowing the type of MCO with which you are dealing can be important in assessing your legal rights and obligations under state or federal law.
3. What services are covered?
4. How are providers compensated?
5. What are the cost-containment mechanisms and utilization-review process?
6. How are referral agreements handled?
7. Is there a provider directory?
8. Is there a "hold-harmless" clause that shifts liability from the plan to you?
9. Which hospitals are available for admission of plan subscribers?
10. Is there a gag clause? These clauses say in essence that providers should not "bad mouth" the plan to patients. Therapists should look carefully for such provisions, especially if they prohibit the therapist from advising the patient of the risks and benefits of alternative treatment options. The gag clause in the contract may state that the contract will terminate if the therapist violates the restriction.

☐ Becoming a Provider

Selection and credentialing are part of becoming a provider for an MCO. Some of the areas that might be reviewed during the credentialing process are licensure, relevant education and training, professional work experience, areas of specialization, certifications, hospital privileges, and information about the provider that may affect the provider's ability to deliver care, such as past substance abuse or licensure actions.

The therapist must complete a detailed application. The application typically includes information such as education, training, licensure, and malpractice history.

Here is a sample letter that can be sent proactively to managed-healthcare companies:

Dear _____ ,

I'm writing you to tell you that I am interested in becoming a provider in your program. My credentials are _____ . Certification number or numbers are _____. Enclosed is a copy of my resume and my malpractice insurance. My office is located in _____. I have _____ years of clinical experience. I specialize in the following areas _____. [Mention if sliding scale is offered and why you believe you would be especially helpful to them in providing services to their clients. List organizational memberships. Thank them for attention to the letter and make a statement about looking forward to working with them.]

Sincerely,

Here are a few suggestions to help you get your foot in the door:

1. Call on corporate executives from big companies.
2. Call the personnel director of a major employer near your office.
3. Offer to give a free seminar to local companies on mental health in the workplace.
4. Contact the director of an existing EAP in a local company.
5. Affiliate with an existing community mental-health center.
6. Contact an EAP consulting firm.
7. Develop your own public-relations and advertising material such as brochures and newsletters that help define your practice.

☐ Alternatives to Managed Care

The question has been asked, "Where do we go from here?" How do we survive and grow in the curious state of mental-health care in which we currently find ourselves? Many will join the wave of managed care and ride it out by affiliating when possible and keeping up on the most current information and trends available. Others will find a comfortable mix of private paying clients and agency-referred clients. Still others recommend creating a new wave entirely.

One proponent of a new system and way to approach the managed care crunch is Nick Cummings, PhD, founder of American Biodyne. We consider Dr. Cummings to be the "guru of managed healthcare" for mental-health professionals. Dr. Cummings describes an opportunity for therapists to join together and form groups to compete with the big MCOs. Dr. Cummings says that therapists, for the first time, are forming their own consortiums. Together they can bid 20% lower simply because they do not have to pay the middle man. Dr. Cummings recommends that local groups link up with groups in other areas in order to compete with large national groups.

Carve-outs are a part of this new wave and may become the next phase of managed healthcare. Increasingly employers are carving out their mental-health benefits. Employees who seek benefits for alcohol and drug abuse treatment and mental-health care are being driven out of HMOs into the traditional indemnity plan, which usually results in higher costs to the employer as well as in adverse selection problems. As carve-outs continue to increase, therapists will have an opportunity to provide services separate from MCOs in a way that has not been available in the past.

☐ Keeping Clear Communication

It is important to keep managed-care relationships functioning smoothly and clearly. From talking to other clinicians and our own experience with managed care, we offer a few suggestions to help you when working with managed care personnel. When possible set specific times to be available for case managers to call. Make sure that you are available during those times. Voice mail systems offer additional possibilities for staying out of the "phone tag" game and saving time.

It is important to track your sessions well in order to avoid a last-minute rush for session approval. A convenient way to note session numbers is by putting the session number in your appointment book or your computer. Another aid is to speak with the case manager personally when possible or to designate one office-staff member to fill that role. It is helpful for a case manager to speak with on a regular basis and begin to know someone in your practice.

When you do talk to case managers, be prepared. Save time by having symptoms, diagnoses, notes, and treatment plans ready to discuss when you talk with them. Confirm authorization for service and add a copy of the authorization to the bill. That can be in the form of an authorization number or a copy of the written authorization. Finally, be sure to follow up on all claims.

Part of communicating clearly involves having well-informed treatment goals. Identifying *Diagnostic and Statistical Manual of Mental Disorders* (DSM)[1] criteria for managed care frequently is necessary. Creating specific goals, around an accurate diagnosis with a plan in mind is the best way to get sessions "approved."

Accurate diagnosis forms the cornerstone of effective treatment and treatment plans. The Minnesota Multiphasic Personality Inventory (MMPI) 2 and the Millon Clinical Multiaxial Inventory III are two inventories frequently used by the therapists at PCS. James M. Butcher, PhD, Ralph's primary consultant in the utilization of the MMPI, has contributed the

---

[1] *Diagnostic and Statistical Manual of Mental Disorders,* Fourth Edition (DSM-IV), 1994, American Psychiatric Association, Washington, DC.

following statements concerning the utilization of the MMPI-2 in managed care:

> The MMPI-2 is the most frequently used and most widely researched personality assessment instrument. One of the most important benefits of the use of the MMPI-2 in today's cost-conscious health care system is that it is a relatively low cost and high yield clinical procedure. In an era of litigiousness, practitioners might be challenged as to why a particular intervention was undertaken or not provided. The initial assessment of baseline personality information can serve to justify practice activity. A number of court cases have centered around the importance of a preliminary assessment in offering mental health services. The MMPI-2 can provide important information about clients that can enhance clinical practice, particularly treatment planning.

These are exciting times for independent practice in the mental-health field. Managed care provides challenges as well as gifts to those of us who are professional therapists. It is essential that we remember that our relationships with the MCOs are business ones, and that our services can be terminated at any time. Economic dependence on one or a few MCOs is dangerous. Being too dependent on a few referral resources never makes sense.

We encourage you to work with MCOs when it makes sense and to continue to expand through private paying clients at the same time. You will find the mix that works best for you and have a better chance of staying afloat when other private practitioners have sunk. There are many resources available to help you—books, seminars, workshops, and through the Internet—that feature managed care and the mental-health practice.

PROFESSIONAL IDENTITY

8

CHAPTER

Soloist or Symphony: Structuring the Business

Whether you are a recent graduate or a therapist who is shifting from an agency to a private practice, the question (once you decide to become an independent practitioner) is how to structure your business. One of the advantages of being a therapist in private practice is the variety of structures available to you.

Ralph's practice has evolved and changed many times throughout his career. Being flexible and adaptable will help you weather the changing environment of mental-health care. Being a relatively new therapist, Dorothy wanted to be in private practice without much of the risk that a business entails.

☐ What Kind of Practice?

More and more, group practice or a management-service organization is becoming the norm, but opportunities for solo practice still are available. Our experience, personalities, and perceptions of clients'\needs have led us to prefer a group structure; not all independent practitioners come to the same choice. The notion of group versus solo practice is sometimes misleading. There are numerous arrangements that combine elements of group and solo practice. Although the terms "group" and "solo" sound clearcut, in fact they can be ambiguous. (They also should not be considered synonymous with the legal structures "sole proprietorship" and "partnership" or "corporation.") A solo practice is obviously a single person practicing alone; however, the solo practitioner might share office space and consult with two other therapists. A PPO may look like a group practice but in fact consist of a collection of solo practitioners who practice at separate locations and do not consult among themselves about clients.

Group Practice

A group practice is a clinical entity that may be comprised of practitioners who are employees, contractors, partners, or a loose federation or association. Frequently the group owns all medical records, client lists, and managed-care contracts. An exception would be a loose federation in which all the records belong to the therapist who has those contracts.

Because most group practices operate as one clinical entity, they have the capacity to set rates with managed-care contractors. Revenue generated for all clinical services goes into a common bank account.

Group practices are best positioned for the changes in an evolving market because they are the most efficient. The group can operate as one entity, with fully integrated administrative and clinical services.

The trend toward group practice stems from certain advantages, some inherent and some the result of changes in healthcare systems. Group practice provides a built-in mechanism for consulting with respected colleagues regularly. Many groups schedule clinical meetings to track the progress of and offer advice about clients. Groups also tend to structure themselves along a gradient of experience; for example, a typical group might consist of two senior therapists who have practiced for many years, three therapists of intermediate experience, and one recent graduate. Groups also can represent a much wider range of areas of therapeutic (and marketing!) expertise than a single individual can.

Another inherent advantage to group practice is coverage for clients in the event of illness, vacation, or professional obligation. For those who are concerned with the issue of "turning it off" and getting away from 24-hour responsibility, the backup support provided in a group practice may be an extremely important consideration. The lifestyle we create as independent practitioners easily can represent a 24-hour burden if one does not have adequate backup. Therapists need to be responsible to people from the minute they say, "Hello," until they say, "Goodbye." Your decision to involve yourself with a group is related to the amount of time and energy you are willing to put into your practice.

A group also is more able financially to hire administrative and clerical personnel and purchase the technology to handle the business and financial record keeping, billing and collections, and general office tasks that are necessary but do not generate income directly. As a practitioner, you need to spend your time doing what you do best. What do you do best? Obviously, this is the therapy, but also the practice building. Who else can build your particular practice better than you can? Thus, a general rule for practitioners is to be efficient by delegating tasks in which you are not expert. If you are sharing the expenses for support staff, and if you use the time that you would have spent doing clerical jobs to build your business, not only your portion of the expenses will be efficiently used, but the compensation to you will be immense.

Being part of a group is also useful in networking. We have found that being a part of a group helps those who have difficulty talking about themselves and what they do. By talking about others in your group— their areas of specialization, credentials, new things that you are doing as a group, the newest member, whatever—you imply your own competence and effectiveness. You also increase your chances of getting a referral somewhere along the line. For example, suppose you are a marriage and family therapist with a secondary specialization in chemical addiction. Jane, the person to whom you are talking at a benefit dinner, has no need of your services nor does she know anyone who does; if you were only talking about yourself that would be the end of it. You have talked, however, about the various other therapists in your group, and later Jane talks about your group and passes along the name of your colleague who specializes in biofeedback to Steve, a friend of hers who has chronic pain that cannot be alleviated physically. Steve begins treatment with your colleague. Steve's coworker John (whom Jane does not know) has confided in Steve that he is worried about his son, whom he suspects may be using drugs, and the strain his son's behavior is putting on his marriage. Steve knows of just the person John and his family should see—you!

The most obvious advantage that group practice provides, in the face of changes in healthcare, is the management of liability. Management of liability does not necessarily mean reduction in your vulnerability to malpractice suits. On the one hand, groups may be more vulnerable to cavalier lawsuits because of the "deeper pockets" of a group (assuming for the moment that the group has some sort of joint liability.) On the other hand, group practice may mitigate against justifiable lawsuits because misdiagnosis or inappropriate treatment is less likely. Management of liability would encompass knowledge of liability risks, clear and considered policies, and a mandate that each member be accountable to the group for adherence to those policies.

Another issue associated with the changing nature of healthcare delivery is that of referral sources, specifically from where they will come in the future. Personal reputation and local networks still will form the foundation from which referrals come. However, with the growth of regional and national networks and "megacontract" affiliations, we think an increasing percentage of referrals will result from these sources. Being associated with a group is an obvious advantage—probably a necessity in fact—for obtaining large contracts. Our belief is that people who are well established in solo practice or who are in popular specialties will continue to succeed in solo practice; for new people coming into the field, joining a group practice may make more sense in the future.

There can be some disadvantages in group practice, depending on the type of group. One difficulty normally associated with groups—lack of decision-making control—is not inevitable. The way a group practice is legally and organizationally structured determines the level of control that an individual has. Other problems that are associated with group practice include the possibility of guilt by association. We know of, for example, an alcohol-rehabilitation counselor, director of a group practice, who was arrested and convicted on several driving-under-the-influence charges; the group lost clients and eventually disbanded because the reputation of the group suffered significantly from one individual's behavior. Individual therapists can lose clients if the group disbands. Groups also are susceptible to all of the difficulties inherent in the group process including jealousies, personality conflicts, gossip, scapegoating, and power conflicts.

Solo Practice

The major advantage to solo practice is independence. The therapist determines how many hours and when he or she will work, the number and type of clients, and the extent and type of practice-building activities. Of course, the therapist is solely responsible for all clinical decisions; for some, this is the profound advantage of individual practice. With total independence, however, comes a concomitant responsibility.

For those solo practitioners who practice from their homes, low overhead is also an advantage. For new graduates and transitioning professionals, the home office frequently is perceived as ideal; no additional rent or utilities payments; availability to one's family; no commuting; lower clothing and food budgets; flexibility of schedule; and freedom to engage in other activities at will (recreational, domestic, etc.). But we find this option fraught with difficulties.

Experience has taught many home practitioners that the elements that they perceived as advantages in fact deter the success of their practices. For example, access to family means access to disruption. Availability to alternate activities means availability to distraction. Savings in rent, food, and clothing costs can result in a lessened image of professionalism, at least in the minds of some potential clients and referral sources. Some clients may find it charming to have to step over the kitty litter to get to where they are going; others will say, "Oh, no!"

Some practitioners believe that client involvement in the therapist's personal surroundings disrupts the formation of transference. If other family members are present, even in a nearby space, the possibility of client restraint in expression of affect is also problematic. Another potential problem centers on lifestyle. Certain therapists practice in one lifestyle and live in another; in the home-based setting, you are opening yourself up to questions, the answers to which you may not want everybody to know. Where you live, how much you spend on your mortgage, or how big or small your house is really is not anyone's business but yours, but if you are practicing at home you are revealing this information whether you want to or not.

Finally, although the risks of personal assault to the practitioner and allegations by the client of impropriety on the part of the therapist are higher for the solo practitioner than for the group practitioner, they are especially salient for the home-based practice. In a home-based setting, if you are dealing with people who are homicidal or suicidal, you are putting yourself and the rest of your family at risk, and there is no way to get around it.

We are not trying to sound uniformly discouraging about the home-based practice. For some people a home-based practice is absolutely what they want, and we say "fine." We also are saying that the decision cannot be based simply on economic considerations: You have to weigh carefully factors such as who your clientele is, who you are attracting, and the image you are putting forth. In addition, many managed-care companies do not contract with practitioners with home-based practices.

Another option that Ralph has encountered to keep overhead low—especially directed toward those fresh from school—is using a referral source's office to see clients, for example, a physician's. Although this arrangement may work on a very short-term basis in individual cases, we believe the overall detriments are greater than the benefits. Again, the general issue of image must be considered. What image are you creating for your client and your referral source by not having your own office? A lack of commitment to independent practice? If you were the physician, how inclined would you be to refer to someone who displaced you from your office—or at least moved your piles of paper and your coffee cup—every time she or he saw a client?

One arrangement that may work, however, is to sublet space from a physician or group of physicians. In this situation, you might be positioning yourself very well for referrals and clerical and administrative support, while keeping your overhead fairly low. Identity issues still might be problematic, however, resulting in a lack of referrals beyond the subletting physicians; privacy might also be a problem. When Ralph began his independent practice (after he had lived in Phoenix long enough to make substantial community contacts), he was associated with a group of obstetrics and gynecology physicians. The group helped him get going and generally become known in town as a practitioner, as well as recognized in the medical community as a family therapist. On the negative side he became known as a person attached to that particular group; that is, other physicians were afraid to refer to him for fear the physicians with whom he was associated might steal the outside referring physicians' clients.

Executive suites offer another possibility for the solo practitioner. These range from a single office to a cluster of offices. Often the buildings offer a package of services from which you can select: clerical, reception, telephone, and computer. Rent is based on size and location of the office, term of the lease, and services chosen. This structure can enhance the appearance of professionalism at a moderate cost. Of course, the traditional choice of the solo practitioner is the self-sustaining arrangement—practitioner and perhaps support staff, in an office within a building occupied by other tenants or occupying its own building.

Business Structure

In legal terms, there are three main types of business organizations—sole proprietorship, partnership, and corporation—with advantages and disadvantages to each, depending on the type of practice and market you have chosen. We are not in the business of giving legal advice. The decision about what business structure is best suited to your needs should only be made in consultation with your tax accountant and an attorney.

Sole Proprietorship

If you are in solo practice, you probably have a sole proprietorship. No organizational documentation is required, and you have absolute authority over all decisions. A sole proprietorship is not taxed as a business entity; business income is taxed as personal income, and losses and expenses are deductible. (Depending on your total income, this taxation procedure can be an advantage or disadvantage.) Upon your death or retirement, there is no formal mechanism required to transfer or sell the practice. What you must remember is that often you must obtain certain types of business-operating licenses. Almost every jurisdiction has some kind of occupational license. You do not need a lawyer to get a license, although you may want to consult with one to find out what licenses are required. The procedure is simple, but failure to obtain a business license could leave you open to a malpractice suit. You also must check zoning requirements, especially if you are practicing or plan to practice in your home. Frequently, a zoning check is part of the business-license procedure, but not necessarily.

A major disadvantage of a sole proprietorship is that it subjects you to unlimited personal liability; if you are sued and the judgment is against you, all of your assets—home, car, personal possessions—may be used in the settlement. This personal liability is of two types: professional, in which you are liable for malpractice if you allegedly err in your practice; and the more general liability of being responsible if someone walks into your office, falls, and breaks a leg. Another main disadvantage of a sole proprietorship is that all profits automatically accrue to the owner, which may put an individual in a very high tax bracket.

Partnership

In a partnership, two or more people agree to share ownership, profits, and sometimes management of a business. Partners can be general or limited. General partners participate in the day-to-day operations of the business and are personally liable for the business's obligations. Limited partners do not participate in management responsibilities or authority and are liable only to the extent of their investment. A partnership must have at least one general partner. Limited partners usually are brought in to provide more capital for the business. For example, you might form a limited partnership with a parent or spouse who agrees to pay the first 6 months' rent on your office in return for a percentage of the profits. As in the sole proprietorship, income in a partnership is taxed as personal income, and losses and expenses are tax deductible.

Partnerships seem to be an area of confusion for therapists. Some form of sharing revenue is the classic test for a partnership, although the sharing does not have to be equal. In the experience of Steven L. Engelberg, who served as legal counsel to the American Association for Marriage and Family Therapy, some therapists may be operating in a relationship that resembles a partnership but is not. Many therapists identify themselves as partners in group practice, but these groups often are more cost-sharing arrangements than partnerships pooling their revenues. Although you do not intend to have a partnership, if you are not careful, there are circumstances under which the law may impose a partnership and its concurrent liability on you. Most states define how a partnership should operate in their jurisdiction. For example, suppose you have an office-sharing arrangement with three other therapist-tenants. You each operate independently, but you share the costs of a secretary, office equipment, and general overhead. You even give yourselves a name, which is technically allowed but can easily, if you are not careful, lead clients, vendors, and so on to believe you are a partnership. In certain cases, state law in effect imposes a partnership on you.

Why should you be concerned if the law considers your arrangement a partnership even if you and your office mates have not drawn up a partnership agreement and do not intend to operate as a partnership? In a partnership, each person is the agent of the other partners; what this means is that you are responsible, liable, for the other's actions. If one person in this arrangement is sued, the others can be named as partners in the lawsuit. If you have chosen to enter into a formal partnership, then you recognize this joint liability up front. You are partners for purposes of professional liability as well as for profits and other commercial purpose. Suppose one general partner orders a $10,000 computer without consulting the others. The others may think the idea a bad one and refuse to pay for the purchase. You are personally liable, however, for each other's actions. Unlike a corporation, a partnership is not a separate, taxable entity. If a partnership is sued or goes bankrupt, the assets are the personal assets of the partners. The partner with more personal assets probably will lose more than those partners with fewer personal assets.

The key factor is how you hold yourself up to the public at large. You cannot present the public with the image that you are a group, all for one and everybody together, if you are not; otherwise, you run the risk of the state imposing its definition of a partnership on you. In other words, you cannot have your cake and eat it, too. If you do not want to run the risk of looking like a partnership, you must make it clear that you all are separate practitioners, even if you operate from a suite of offices with a common reception area. For example, you each put your name outside the main door and individually on your separate offices. You do not hand out literature that suggests you are in business with the other people, and appointments are made separately. If a client calls one of the other therapists, he or she does not get you.

What if you want to draw up a formal partnership agreement? You should consult a lawyer who is familiar with partnership law in the state in which you practice to draw up an agreement spelling out the specifics of the arrangement. (In some states, you must draw up such an agreement to avoid violating state law.) There are certain issues that must be addressed, or you may invoke the default provisions of state-determined partnership laws. These issues vary by state. One area you probably need to define is decision making. You can have a partnership with one dominant partner if you so desire, or you can decide to have a one-person, one-vote arrangement. If you do not spell this out in the agreement the state may declare, for example, that the decision making is by majority vote. Similarly, state law may declare that partnership profits are to be shared equally. Again, other arrangements may be perfectly acceptable, but they must be spelled out in writing. (There are such things as oral partnerships, but they sometimes are very difficult to enforce.)

Another issue that needs to be dealt with in a formal partnership is continuity. In many states, the death or withdrawal of one partner automatically dissolves the entire partnership. If you are in partnership with more than one person, you obviously do not want this to happen, so again you must specify in writing what happens in the event of death or withdrawal of one partner.

Of course the main issue involved in a partnership is one we have already mentioned: liability. Each general partner is your agent and literally can bind you and the partnership to whatever acts he or she carries out, including alleged professional malpractice. Traditionally, therapists who prescribe medication, usually psychiatrists, have been sued more frequently and for greater amounts than those who practice the so-called talking therapies. Thus, the fact that you can be sued for someone else's act may be more important because of the threat of lawsuits in the first place, and not necessarily because of ultimate judgments and amounts.

Deciding whether or not the benefits of a partnership outweigh the potential problems with liability is an individual decision. We emphatically recommend that you engage a lawyer to draw up a partnership agreement if you do decide to form a partnership. She or he can advise you about what issues should be covered and various alternatives to standard arrangements that can be tailored to your particular practice. Your professional life is too important to play amateur lawyer. One of the points that we have repeated throughout this book is to do what you do best and build a team for yourself that includes the services of others doing what they do best.

Incorporation

One of the primary reasons for incorporating is to shield yourself from liability. Unlike sole proprietorships and partnerships, corporations are autonomous legal entities. Ownership of a corporation is freely transferable, and a corporation does not cease to exist if the owner or partners die. Most salient is the provision that the liability of each shareholder usually is limited to the amount he or she has invested. The bad news is that there is a fundamental difference between a professional business and a nonprofessional business: professionals cannot shield themselves from professional liability (malpractice) by incorporating. Many states have specific laws that allow professionals to incorporate and spell out ways in which incorporation should be handled. Other states do not have such laws.

In neither case are you necessarily protected from the threat of suit. For example, suppose you are in solo practice but want to set yourself up as a corporation. (State regulations vary on whether or not this is allowed.) Assuming for the moment your state does allow this, you file the proper legal documents and add "Inc." or "LLC" to the name of your practice. A client decides to sue you for alleged inappropriate diagnosis and treatment. You probably cannot respond by saying, "Wait, I'm off the hook. I'm not individually liable because I'm incorporated." In Engelberg's opinion, the court is more likely to say, "Tough." You are an individual professional performing services. You cannot hide behind a corporate shield." This is a very different situation from a plumber coming into your house, running amuck, and being as negligent as possible. If the plumber is properly incorporated and properly maintaining a corporation, you probably cannot sue the plumber but must go after the corporation.

If you are a solo practitioner, reasons to incorporate most likely focus on certain tax considerations. To figure out your individual situation, we advise you to consult with a good accountant. Many of the traditional tax advantages for corporations have fallen by the wayside as a result of changes in tax law. Subsequent tax-reform activity may or may not alter your particular situation.

Sub-Chapter S

An intermediate structure between a corporation and a partnership is the "sub–chapter S" corporation. Sub–S corporations are small corporations with a limited number of stockholders. In this structure, the corporation is taxed like a partnership; that is, the corporation's incomes or losses are credited or debited to the stockholders in proportion to their holdings, and there is no taxation at the corporate level. The sub–S corporation also protects you against personal (nonprofessional) liability and may offer some tax advantages regarding long-term capital gains. The value of this structure for your business is best decided by you and your attorney.

In Engelberg's opinion, if you are in solo practice, whether or not you incorporate is probably not a "life or death" situation, although he cautions that each person should make this decision only in consultation with his or her lawyer. If you are practicing as a group and you intend to operate like a partnership, you may want to consider forming a corporation, because there are certain ways of incorporating that facilitate decision making, continuity, and other issues discussed in the section on partnerships. Also, please be aware that, in certain states, if you plan to incorporate a group, you are going to have difficulty combining some professions in this corporation. In some states, a psychologist can only form a partnership with another licensed psychologist. In other states, multidisciplinary corporations are legal. We reiterate: As a practicing professional, decisions about whether or not you can incorporate, and whether or not you should, require sensitive legal judgment; unless you can afford to be cavalier in your decision, we recommend that you consult a business attorney for advice.

☐ Begin To Define Your Business Structure

By answering the following questions you begin to define your preferences for business structure. We think it is helpful to project yourself into a variety of scenarios in order to see which type of practice is best suited for your practice:

1. If you were to be in a solo practice, what would that look like? Write out the ideal situation that you would like to have, answering questions like: Would you share office space, will you consult with other therapists, how will after-hours calls be handled, and so forth. Refer back to the section on solo practice as you define your own structure.
2. If you were to be in a group practice, what would that look like? Again, write out the ideal situation as you define a group structure, answering questions like: How many therapists in your group, will they have different specialties, who makes decisions, how is conflict handled, how are referrals to the group assigned, what will the legal entity look like, and so forth. Refer back to the section on group practice as you define your own structure.

After you have written out your ideal business structure, evaluate the different aspects in terms of present-day availability and feasibility. Note whether some of the features could be worked out through future planning.

CHAPTER

From Design to Detail: Office Planning, Policies, and Procedures

Your office is a statement of your marketing and therapeutic image. The location, design, and furniture communicate definite ideas about your approach to the practice of therapy and business to those who visit. For example, the Gestalt therapist's office frequently has props, pillows, additional chairs, and space for moving about. The more traditional office might be furnished with a desk with a chair on either side. A 3-inch plush carpet might suggest how you are spending your fee. You need to assess the impact of these statements on your particular market. What might be expected or reassuring to some clients may be threatening or annoying to others.

One idea that we believe is a myth—or a mistake—is the notion of, "Well, I'd like to have an office that fits in with a certain level of clientele (those who can afford to pay), but I'm just starting out and can't swing the overhead, so I'll start with low overhead (for example, office in the home or in a certain geographic location, secondhand or inadequate furniture) and change to a higher overhead (a more distinctive office) when my practice is established." The problem with this idea is that changing the image established by your first office may be tougher and take longer than you think. If you try to cut overhead too much when you are beginning and project a certain image, through subsequent referrals and feedback that image may follow you in the community for a long time.

☐ Location

Location is the first consideration for your office's image. Common sense tells us to consider such factors as adequate parking, convenience to the target market, easy access to main thoroughfares and bus lines, ambiance of the neighborhood, and zoning regulations. A demographic study might be useful in making decisions about office location. Ralph's facility, for example, is located one block away from Scottsdale Hospital, one of the main general hospitals in Scottsdale, and a block-and-a-half from the Samaritan Behavioral Health Center. The area serves as a hub for the entire valley, and referrals come from Phoenix, Tempe, Mesa, Scottsdale, Chandler, Gilbert, and Glendale.

Furnishings are another important consideration in planning your office. In thinking about furnishings for your office—this idea also pertains to location—keep in mind that the space in which you practice must be a background, and not an interruption, to the therapeutic process. It may be helpful to think of furnishing your office in a way that somehow reflects the lifestyle of your clients and fits into the neighborhood environment surrounding your office. You convey messages both of who you are and who your clients are with art, color, furniture style, and plants; even the magazines in your waiting room convey images of you and your clients.

Both of us believe in creating a flexible, comfortable, living-room setting; that is our bias based on our identities as marriage and family therapists. As we have mentioned, context is everything—hot tubs would be a bit too relaxed and casual for our particular clientele, as would the 40-year-old, overstuffed chairs with the stuffing coming out from Aunt Mathilde's attic. And you do not want to charge $85, $100, $200 an hour and make your clients sit on stools and folding chairs. At the same time, creating an office that looks like something from a penthouse suite in New York (unless you happen to practice among the very well-to-do in New York) also may be a poor choice. You do not want your clients to resent your fee because they think it all is going into plush carpeting and collectors' items.

☐ Support Services and Staff

Support services in your office are critical, especially surrounding the telephone. Our personal preference is to have a person answering the phone as opposed to other types of phone contact. That is not always affordable to someone starting out in a private practice. Our hierarchy of choice would be (from least desirable to most):

1. Having an answering machine
2. Having an answering machine and a beeper
3. Using a voicemail system
4. Utilizing an answering service
5. Employing a support person to be on site during office hours

Even if you are on a tight budget and are looking for the lowest possible overhead, we believe an answering service, and not an answering machine, is preferable. You do not want to come back to a machine and hear, "142 pills at 3:42 on Friday afternoon and goodbye," and it is now Wednesday and a lawyer wants to know what kind of coverage you have and who is responsible. Not all answering services are alike, however, and a poor one is almost as bad as having none at all. Before you sign up with any service, ask these questions:

1. Who are your customers? Are any of them therapists?
2. Will you provide 24-hour coverage?
3. Will the same people handle my calls or will they be answered randomly? What is the average length of employment of your employees?
4. May I select the people who handle my calls and train them?
5. Does your staff handle emergency situations for other clients?
6. What is the protocol for calling me? How quickly will I be called?
7. May I script your staff's responses to my calls and rehearse them?
8. How are fees determined—flat fee, per call, or another way?

If these questions seem overly detailed or picky, remember that the person answering your telephone creates the first impression of your business (meaning, you) in the minds of clients, potential clients, and referral sources. You may be the best therapist in the world, but if your initial contact via the telephone with the public is unpleasant, less than professional, or incompetent, you will never have the opportunity to practice therapy on any client.

Once you have selected a service and you visit the facility to sign the contract, we suggest that you humanize the relationship. For example, bring the answering service staff cookies or fruit or flowers on occasion; learn the names of the staff. You may want to make periodic visits to the service because of employee turnover. You also may want to arrange for a friend or colleague to call your service occasionally and offer you feedback. You want the service personnel to realize that you are serious and professional about what you do. In turn, they will treat your clients with respect and dignity and extend your professional image. When we are treating people with real dilemmas, we need support staff who perceive emergencies as genuine.

We recognize that not all therapists are able to find an acceptable answering service, and some choose to use voice mail. If you do, your message should reflect your professionalism and concern. Clients find it helpful when the message contains information about when you will be available and how often you check your voice mail. You also may want to include an emergency number at which you, a colleague, or hospital emergency staff with whom you have a coverage arrangement can be reached.

Here is the message Ralph currently uses for his practice when his office manager is unable to take the call:

> Hello, you have reached Psychological Counseling Services. Our office hours are from 8:00 to 5:00 Monday through Thursday, and from 8:00 to 3:00 on Fridays. If you have reached this message during scheduled hours, we are either away from our desk or on another line. If this is an emergency and you are trying to reach a therapist, please hang up and dial 911 or a crisis center. If you need to cancel an appointment, you may leave your name and number and the time that you called. If you want to schedule an appointment, you will need to call back. Thank you.

Many therapists are choosing to carry beepers, at least part of the time. Beepers can be used for emergency calls or for therapists who want their clients to have access to them 24 hours a day.

If you are in a practice that can support a receptionist or secretary, the same principles apply. It is your responsibility to make sure your staff not only represents you in a friendly, concerned, and professional manner but is trained to truly support your efficacy as a practitioner. This is particularly true if they are called on to recognize and react to emergencies. A staff member's compassion and willingness to act can save the client's life. Staff members also need to be aware of boundaries between the therapist and the front office.

We are biased in favor of having at least one full-time support person if you are in full-time independent practice. A secretary, office manager, or receptionist can tie many threads together. She or he can be the original contact person both on the phone and in person, thus creating a comfortable sense of continuity for the client. Handling the phones is especially important when you are in session. We know some therapists who take all calls themselves, even while they are in session. Some are able to do this tactfully. We do not feel that this is in the clients' best interests, because it disrupts the special relationship therapy represents. In addition, a secretary or bookkeeper can be responsible for making contractual billing and payment arrangements with clients, freeing the therapist from that role. We believe support staff more than pay for themselves, in that the therapist gains additional time to take on more clients and engage in activities to market the business that actually result in payback, rather than spending his or her time on nonpaid administrative tasks.

If you are in private practice part-time, obviously a full-time support person may not make much sense. We urge you to consider hiring a support person in conjunction with other therapists or other professionals. For instance, you could arrange with two other colleagues in part-time independent practice—not necessarily in the same location, although proximity would be useful—to divide the services of one full-time person. Perhaps you would have the secretary for 15 hours a week, your colleague for another 15 hours, and the third colleague for 10. Employee benefits and required contributions such as FICA, unemployment insurance, and worker's compensation can be split along percentages tied to the proportions of hours. We caution you to consult with your attorney about this arrangement if there is any question of implied partnership.

☐ Computers in the Therapist's Office

Computers are a great asset for any business including a professional therapy practice. There are two main types of computer applications for the therapist's office: clerical and clinical.

Clerical applications handle such functions as word processing, billing, accounting, scheduling, and administrative reporting. Some software packages developed specifically for therapists' clerical tasks focus on insurance and billing procedures, because these areas are complicated for a therapy practice. Other packages integrate scheduling, billing, and accounting functions. There are a number of advantages good software can provide including savings in staff costs, consistency in office practice, professionalism, and business planning.

Computers offer a variety of clinical applications as well as clerical. These clinical applications include such tasks as assigning diagnoses, gathering client data, conducting biofeedback, utilizing cognitive retraining, and administering and scoring psychological tests. In addition, the use of the Internet and E-mail to consult with other professionals or conduct research is a great resource for any practitioner.

☐ Fees, Payment, Billing, and Collections

Steven Engelberg, the attorney whom we mentioned in a previous chapter, offers an interesting perspective on the issue of money (fees, billing, collections) and its relationship to the helping side of our profession. He says, speaking of his profession and of ours,

I believe we have a duty to do more than make money; we also have a duty to give something back. We all have a duty to do pro bono work, but one reason we often don't prefer to do pro bono work is that we are wasting our time with a lot of people who can afford to pay and don't pay, people who won't deal with us in a commercially fair way. In your commercial time, make sure you are commercial. Don't lose what you have earned (from those who can afford to pay) to unreasonably low fee-setting or sloppy billing and collection.

The therapist has an ethical duty to be very clear about what is expected of the client concerning the entire financial procedure—from clearly delineated fees to the billing, payment, and collection arrangements. Certainly this is important as a protection against litigation. Many therapists also believe payment issues to be important to the therapeutic process. The therapist, after clearly spelling out the terms—how much and when—then must expect that the client will fulfill her or his part of the contract and also must make that expectation clear to the client. Finally, the therapist must follow up with the client along the lines of the original agreement.

Setting Fees

There is nothing hard and fast about the first part of the process, setting fees. You need to gather as much data as you can about fee structures. Professional publications periodically give national fee structures and averages. Data on particular types of therapists (psychiatrists, counselors, psychologists, or marriage and family therapists, for example) usually are available from professional organizations. You also should contact local colleagues in your area of specialization, because particular geographic areas may differ widely from the average. For example, a city with a disproportionately high number of counselors may support a lower-than-average fee; this situation may be modified, however, for a particular therapist if she or he has a subspecialty not well represented in this city.

Finally, you should contact third-party payers to find out what their maximum allowances are. Keep in mind, however, that you may want to set your fees higher than third-party payers currently allow, because fee scales for a given year frequently are based on the median fees from the previous year.

If you want to raise your fees, the same kind of homework is useful. Some therapists raise their fees only for new clients, keeping current clients at the fee at which they began. This can create record-keeping and billing nightmares and increase the chances that you will bill some clients in error, all of which can contribute to collection problems. We find it preferable to begin telling all of your current clients, at least 3 months in advance, that you will be raising your fees. In our experience, most clients are amenable to the change if they have sufficient notice to prepare for it. As they come in, new clients also are told up front of the impending change.

Therapists who are just beginning in the field or who are new to independent practice often are tempted to set fairly low fees. Although this is an individual decision and can sometimes bolster a practice (as, for example, if you work out an arrangement with a senior practitioner whereby he or she regularly sends you clients referred to him or her who cannot afford that practitioner's fees), in our experience, we find it preferable to set fees comparable to our colleagues' fee structures. We believe that this is important to your own sense of self-worth as well as to your professional image and standing among your colleagues.

In general, payment can take the form of cash (check), charge (VISA, MasterCard, etc.), or insurance. Although accepting charge cards represents an additional cost to Ralph's practice, he has found that it encourages patient responsibility for payment.

As in any service business, cancellations and no-shows can disrupt anticipated cash flow. The therapist needs to establish a clear payment policy for missed appointments. In Ralph's practice, if people do not cancel 24 hours in advance, they are charged a full fee. Some therapists charge half fees, and some do not charge. Ralph states,

> I want, as that person's therapist (and it's never the secretary who makes the decision), to make the decision not to charge if the client has a good reason for not showing up. It's interesting that we have seldom had a problem with the insurance company for a situation where we charge for a session and the patient didn't come. We talked to some insurance carriers about it. We put down the fee and 'no show' and sometimes they pay for it and sometimes they don't. I don't want to end up with a collection agency or in Small Claims Court because of those sessions. The other side is that we get 75 to 80 percent of the claims paid anyway—full fee. Our clients understand that if they don't call to cancel ahead of time, other professionals besides therapists will charge for their time.

A final caveat about setting fees: Do not charge clients with insurance a fee different from what you charge those without insurance. You also should not waive copayments as a general policy. In certain cases, courts have ruled these practices to be insurance fraud. You always have the option to reduce the fee or waive the copayment for a particular client.

Collections

There is disagreement among therapists about whether or not the business of payment and collections is part of the therapeutic process. In Ralph's practice—another advantage of a group—Ralph has a comptroller: a bookkeeper who gives clients a specific standardized contract, which they sign, that says, "I agree to pay at each session." If they cannot do this, they work out a payment plan with the bookkeeper. The bookkeeper also is responsible for collections, thus adding continuity to the process. From the beginning, the contract makes clear what the client will pay each month.

At some point you may want to consider using a collection agency or going to Small Claims Court. Ralph indicates clearly on his fee contract that his group sometimes uses a collection agency. You need to weigh the costs of going either of these routes against the expected return (leaving aside for the moment the issue of intangible returns.) A collection agency usually charges a percentage of whatever it collects, and this percentage varies with the size of the account and your business in general.

Small Claims Court is usually (depending on local laws) for claims of damages less than a set amount. Serving the papers usually costs an additional fee, the amount of which depends on whether the papers can be served through the mail or require a process server. Ralph has been to Small Claims Court only two or three times. "One time happened to be for a guy who I walked out my back door to his Mercedes. The guy said, 'I've been owing you [whatever the amount was] for a long time, eventually I'll get it paid.' I was thinking, 'They haven't repossessed your car.' So we ended up in Small Claims. The hearing officer said, 'Are you disputing the services by Dr. Earle? Did he perform those services?' The guy said, 'I'm not disputing it at all—I think he did a good job. He was very helpful.' The officer said, 'Well, pay your bill.' Sometimes being tough is important. In our case, because we're a group, we have somebody else (in our case, a comptroller, but it could be another therapist) be tough for us."

Third-Party Payment

Third-party payments are those provided by an insurer. If you follow the following suggestions, your third-party payments should go smoothly most of the time. Collecting your fees directly from patients is the best approach. Although you want to do everything feasible to get third parties to pay on claims, you do not want to be left holding the bag if proper reimbursement is not paid out.

Reassure patients about confidentiality, as it is a very common worry, especially if forms are routinely filed with a company's personnel department. Many personnel offices now bend over backwards on confidentiality; most plans offer the option of direct filing with insurance firms.

Make sure your office takes extra care with claim forms. Whether you or a secretary files them, it pays to give them a final review before you sign and put them in the mail. Getting all data down accurately and legibly saves everyone endless trouble.

It is important to know diagnostic language and how to apply it to your patient. Despite worries about confidentiality, you have to provide an accurate and understandable diagnosis to get claims paid. A good source of diagnostic terms is the current edition of the *Diagnostic and Statistical Manual of Mental Disorders* from the American Psychiatric Association.

Never fudge on your credentials. Many plans will not pay some types of providers, and that tempts some therapists to get physicians and licensed clinical psychologists to sign claim forms for them. This not only can lead to legal problems but also to suits for repayment of fees. It is better to file for reimbursement under your own professional credentials and then fight rejection with evidence of your degrees, license, register listing, and so forth. Services provided in an "approved clinic" often qualify for reimbursement, even if the company or agency does not consider you an approved service provider.

File your claims at the right time, and avoid waiting too long to start. One provider waited until a claim had reached $16,000 before sending it on to the insurance carrier. Remember that some contracts disallow claims filed more than a year after service, and although that often is not enforced, late claims usually lead to extra scrutiny. In most cases, it can be a good idea to file the first claim as soon as possible, or, if there is a deductible, as soon as that figure has been reached on the account. Another mistake is sending in bills too frequently, or on an erratic schedule—that means extra work for you. Sending in a form on a monthly basis is a practical policy.

Finally there is the issue of signing off. If you are licensed, you can sign the insurance form, adding your title and license number. Many times the carrier will pay because you are a licensed provider. It is also standard practice to sign the forms as the treating provider and have someone else sign as the supervising provider if the relationship between you is truly supervisory. A supervisory relationship is defined and determined by the norms of your profession and not by law.

Some groups do not identify the treating provider on the claims form but instead use only the supervisor's or clinical director's name. The role of each person who appears on the form must be delineated. If you are signing off on others' claims, do not claim to be the supervisor or the treating provider unless you actually are, or you could be held liable. Whatever facts appear on the insurance form must be true.

☐ Financial Planning

We previously have discussed the importance of having various professionals available for consulting about clients' needs. It is equally important to have professional consultants for your needs. These consultants might include attorneys, accounting and tax professionals, and financial planners and managers. Unless you have the time, aptitude, and inclination to become expert in a number of fields, their services are indispensable. Hiring consultants is not necessarily costly. Not hiring them can be.

Cultivating contacts before they actually are needed prevents operating from a crisis mentality. Successful businesses, regardless of the field, plan ahead—and planning ahead requires that you extend networking efforts beyond your profession. Advance planning also allows you to interview a variety of professionals to determine with whom you can best work. It is likely that you eventually will need access to more than one individual in a given field. For example, the attorney who assists you in setting up your corporation may not be able to do your practice audit or advise you on malpractice issues. Although the following checklist of professional activities may seem obvious, many practitioners have confided in us that when they first began their practices, they were sometimes unsure about whom to see for what. You will notice some overlap in services provided by the various advisors:

Accountant: Basic financial planning (money management, investment opportunities and counseling), tax planning and preparation, establishment of financial records and record keeping, and general business planning (decisions about expansion, incorporation).

Attorney: General legal counsel (litigation, liability, practice audit, contract negotiation), decisions about business structure, malpractice advice, general business and financial planning, initiation of collection procedures, personal legal counsel (wills, estate planning).

Financial planners: Money management, investment planning and counseling, brokerage services, retirement and estate planning, insurance, buy and sell agreements.

Marketing specialists: Market research, brochures, strategies for expansion of practice, positioning, strategic planning for the future.

Public relations and advertising specialists: Media placement, speaking engagements, interviews, advertising consultation, publicity.

Insurance: Life insurance, overhead-expense insurance, disability income insurance and major medical or hospitalization coverage, and casualty or liability insurance.

Payroll Taxes

If your practice includes any employees beyond partners or independent consultants and contractors, your financial planning requires attention to costs incurred by FICA (social security), federal and state withholding taxes, unemployment insurance, worker's compensation, and, where applicable, state disability insurance. These are federally or state-regulated programs; ignoring them is the easiest way to find yourself quickly out of business.

Tax Planning

In considering your tax situation we suggest attention to the following pertinent categories: business deductions for items such as home office and equipment expenses; automobile expenses; business-related travel; educational expenses; entertainment expenses; certain kinds of finance charges; deferment of income or payments; and depreciation. Another major area concerns retirement planning. The best sources of information are your accountant, financial planner, attorney, insurance agent, and banker.

Vital to tax planning is good record keeping. First, you need to establish what financial information is required for your general business assessment and planning and then develop the most efficient system for recording and organizing that information. Information must be recorded regularly. Payroll and accounting services set up and maintain your records as well as handle the paperwork required for compliance with regulations. Many practitioners find these services time-saving and cost-effective. Next, we discuss your practice and the law.

Your Practice and the Law: Legal Liability and Protection

More than ever before, the therapist must retain an attorney with expertise in therapy-practice law in the cadre of consultants. Clients are more likely to litigate than in the past; therapists are more likely to be asked to testify in a trial, have their records subpoenaed, or be held accountable for certain of their clients' behaviors. This chapter highlights some of the most common and confusing legal issues that therapists may face. This confusion arises from multiple causes: The courts are attempting to formulate guidelines for ethical practice at least in part based on legal decisions, and individual therapists are attempting to apply a general law to specific situations and to balance their interpretation of laws and guidelines with their therapeutic instincts, which may conflict. The second part of the chapter focuses on ways in which you can protect yourself against liability even in the midst of ever-changing legal guidelines and decisions.

We cannot emphasize enough the importance of consulting your own attorney about these issues. Our discussion intends to alert you to potential legal difficulties; it is not intended as legal advice. These difficulties can be arranged into three categories: confidentiality, dual relationships, and negligence.

☐ Confidentiality

Confidentiality is critical to the therapist-client relationship. For that reason, it also is the area in which the therapist is exposed to the greatest liability. The range of confidentiality extends from the content of a therapy session to the fact that a given client is being seen. Although it is no less sacred to them than the priest's Seal of Confession, therapists now are asked more frequently to violate their mandate of client confidentiality. The reasons are myriad, including court action, potentially dangerous clients, and professional impropriety. The following fictitious case studies illustrate two confidentiality dilemmas.

Janelle is a therapist in independent practice who specializes in geriatrics. She often is referred clients from an inpatient facility. She had been seeing Carrie for approximately 1 month. At a recent session, Carrie threatened to kill her sister Louisa who had tried to have her committed. Janelle broke confidentiality by notifying Louisa and the local police of her threat. Carrie did not follow through with her threat but subsequently sued Janelle for breach of confidentiality. The judge upheld Janelle's duty to warn Louisa and the police and dismissed the suit.

Christopher is a marriage and family therapist in independent practice in a metropolitan area. His client, Jeffrey, was a recovering alcoholic who had been sober for 3 years. Jeffrey had been involved in an automobile accident and was sued. The plaintiff's attorney petitioned Christopher to testify. The attorney did not know of Jeffrey's history of alcoholism, and the defense attorney, obviously, was concerned that he not discover it. At the trial, when questioned by the plaintiff's attorney, Christopher refused to answer any questions relating to Jeffrey, citing his obligation to maintain confidentiality. The judge in this case let Christopher's position stand.

Waivers of Confidentiality

Only a client can waive confidentiality. The therapist must maintain confidentiality unless an exception applies. To waive confidentiality, a patient should sign a release form. Waiving confidentiality for one purpose, however, does not mean the privilege necessarily is waived for some other purpose. To protect themselves, therapists should obtain signed releases for each circumstance and update them periodically. Therapists who work with families should follow the guideline of the American Association for Marriage and Family Therapy that each family member who is legally competent must agree to waive confidentiality in order to release information about any individual member. Again, this is a crucial issue and sometimes may require the assistance of a legal expert.

Subpoenas

Because you have received a subpoena does not necessarily mean that the therapist-client privilege is waived. Initial subpoenas have nothing to do with whether or not the court has decided to waive privilege; they are merely one party's demand for information. Although a therapist must respond to a properly served subpoena, his or her response asserts the client's privilege unless an exception applies. A subpoena is merely a document directing you to go to a certain place. It may tell you to bring certain records, and if it does, you must bring these records and appear to testify. A subpoena does not necessarily require you to testify, but merely to show up. If you are subpoenaed by your client's attorney, your only precaution might be to request that your client sign a waiver. If you receive a subpoena from someone other than your client's attorney, your first obligation is to inform your client that someone is trying to obtain information. Consult your client's attorney if asked to do so. You may give the requested information if your client signs a waiver of confidentiality. If your client does not waive confidentiality, there are a number of ways, in some part depending on state law, to quash the subpoena, and you should consult your or your client's attorney about how to do so.

The therapist should alert the client about the ramifications of waiving. For example, your file may contain information about the client that is potentially embarrassing or incriminating. If the client waives confidentiality and calls you as a witness, your file can be examined by the other side, and you are subject to cross-examination about it. If you attempt to hold anything back from that file, you may find yourself in legal trouble. Once confidentiality is waived, the other side has the right to see and use everything.

If you are asked to testify, it is not your job to go to court and change the facts, withhold information, alter your records, or hold back records. If you do any of these, you could be accused of obstructing justice. If you are ordered by the judge to testify—and remember that this is not the same as an initial subpoena—it is your duty to testify and bring with you all records if so ordered and not to mislead, misrepresent, or perjure yourself in any way.

If you are subpoenaed to be a witness—whether as an "expert" witness, without prior agreement, or on your own behalf in a malpractice action—there are a few general guidelines that have been recommended by the American Association for Marriage and Family Therapy.

1. Many therapists feel intimidated into changing answers. If you are not sure of your answers, say so.
2. It is essential to review your records carefully. It is very embarrassing to say something that is in direct contradiction to your own records.
3. Staying clearly with the questions asked is essential. Frequently, therapists fall in the trap of providing information that is not needed and sometimes not relevant to the questions. The courtroom is not a place for personal speculation.

4. The proper authorization is needed for all disclosure. A subpoena does not waive the privilege that protects the therapist–client communication. It is essential that the guidelines of the ethics of your professional association(s) and state legislative guidelines be followed. Sometimes it is helpful to get direction from the judge. When in doubt it is always better to err on the cautious side and to consult with other colleagues and/or a malpractice attorney when needed.

5. Nothing is gained by giving quick answers. It is essential to listen to the question and reflect about the answer. Sometimes objections may be made to the question before an answer is given.

6. Truth telling is critical in your answers. Your task is to be candid and let the chips fall where they may.

7. It does make sense to practice cross-examination with the attorney who has subpoenaed you. This rehearsal is not unethical and actually is helpful in reducing anxiety. If you have never testified in a court before, it may make sense to visit a courtroom and/or sit in on another trial in order to become more comfortable with that venue. Also, it is frequently helpful to role-play a courtroom process with colleagues. Remember, anxiety is very normal in such situations.

8. If you have published books or journal articles relevant to the material being dealt with in the case, it is critical to be aware of statements made by you in those publications. Too many of our colleagues have been caught off guard when they hear the words off the printed page brought up in court. If you have changed you mind about certain areas since publication, then it is important to defend the reasons for such changes.

9. Any materials coming out of a deposition done by you are fair game for use in court. Contradictions by you as a witness in court are highly likely to be used to disprove your credibility.

10. Testifying in court is not a place to become defensive. Sometimes, attorneys will attempt to make the therapist angry or defensive. The goal is to remain centered and focused.

Your time on the stand should be less than the time you spend preparing. Do not be surprised if your case is set for trial and rescheduled one or more times. Nor is it uncommon for litigants to settle just prior to trial. Last-minute settlements can be both a relief and disappointment to witnesses.

Mandatory Reporting

Under mandatory-reporting statutes, states require that therapists break confidentiality at times. These statutes generally concern child abuse and neglect. Every state has child-abuse reporting laws, although the laws differ. Some states require that you personally observe some evidence of abuse; other states require that you have some knowledge of the abuse. These laws often apply across the board to all types of helping professionals, and there are very stringent criminal penalties for failure to report. For your protection, as well as that of your clients, it is imperative that you find out your state's requirements for mandatory reporting and keep informed about how the laws are interpreted by the courts. Therapists should be aware that failure to comply with mandatory-reporting statutes may result in private civil liability as well as state-imposed sanctions.

Duty to Warn and Duty to Protect

This law has recognized certain situations in which preventing harm supersedes maintaining confidentiality. These laws concern third parties who may be at risk, as well as the patient. The specifics of these situations are discussed in the section on negligence.

☐ Dual Relationships

Aside from confidentiality issues, the most common cause of a professional liability claim against a therapist concerns dual relationships. Because of the trust and dependency established in therapy, the law has mandated that clients receive special protection against exploitation by the therapist. Such exploitation may take the form of sexual intimacy between therapists and clients, as well as other forms.

As more attention has been focused on this issue, professional groups are attempting to develop clear guidelines on the subject. Many state statutes governing professional conduct make sexual contact between therapist and client grounds for disciplinary action. Such contact after termination of therapy also may result in malpractice claims and disciplinary proceedings.

Therapists should recognize that some insurance companies do not cover malpractice suits concerning sexual contact. At best, they may cover defense costs. Many insurance carriers take the position that a battery, or wrongful touching, is an act of commission, not one of negligence. It is within the purview of the insurance company to protect the therapist only in cases of negligence.

The issue of dual relationships is not confined to sexual relationships between therapists and patients. There are many questions that remain about what constitutes an appropriate or inappropriate dual relationship. Although there may be a case here or a statute there dealing with a specific situation, many of these dual-relationship issues have not been addressed systematically by the law. For example, although we all might agree that hiring a current client to be a receptionist in one's office is clearly inappropriate, what about hiring that person some years after termination of therapy? Answers to this kind of question currently come from consensus among therapists in a given community or within a given professional group. These answers vary from group to group and area to area. We emphasize again the need to educate, and continually reeducate, yourself about the norms in your community and your profession.

☐ Negligence

The concept of negligence arose from the notion that, under certain circumstances, a person has a legal duty toward someone else. If this duty is violated and if an injury results from this violation, then the person who did not carry out his or her duty properly may be guilty of negligence. Negligence actions against physicians usually focus on inappropriate diagnosis or treatment. Negligence claims against a therapist are still fairly rare and generally involve treatment of dangerous patients, specifically with regard to the therapist's duty to warn and duty to protect.

Duty to Warn

In August 1969 a man who was a voluntary outpatient at the student health service on a university campus was in counseling with a psychologist. The patient had confided to his psychologist his intention to kill an unnamed woman (who was readily identifiable) when she returned from an extended trip. In consultation with other university counselors, the psychologist made the assessment that the patient was dangerous and should be committed to a mental hospital for observation. The psychologist later called the campus police and told them of the death threat and of his conclusion that the patient was dangerous. The campus officers did take the patient into custody for questioning, but they later released him when he gave evidence of being "rational" and promised to stay away from the woman. He was never confined to a treatment facility. The psychologist followed up his call with a formal letter requesting the assistance of the chief of the campus police. Later, the psychologist's supervisor asked that the letter be returned, ordered that the letter and the psychologist's case notes be destroyed, and asked that no further action be taken in the case. It should be noted that the woman and her family were never made aware of this potential threat. Shortly after the woman's return from her trip, the patient killed her. Her parents filed suit against the Board of Regents and employees of the university for having failed to notify the intended victim of the threat. The State Supreme Court ruled in favor of the parents, holding that a failure to warn an intended victim was professionally irresponsible.

If there is a choice between violating confidentiality and protecting a third party from getting killed or injured, court decisions seem to indicate that you must err on the side of warning. The problem is, though, if you act too precipitously, you could find yourself involved in a serious lawsuit.

Frequently, foreseeability of harm is a major factor in cases involving suicidal or dangerous patients. A physician's or therapist's ability to control a patient's behavior is another important factor. All therapists, nevertheless, must be cognizant of the laws and their potential liability in treating dangerous or suicidal patients.

Duty to Protect

Unlike duty to warn, which mandates that the therapist consider third parties threatened by patients, duty to protect involves the therapist's responsibility and the limits to her or his legal liability in cases of patients who are dangerous to themselves. Duty to protect is variously known as *duty to prevent* or *duty to commit*. This duty is tricky because you are dealing with a suicidal person. Therapists, both for humanitarian and legal reasons, are in danger if they sit by passively and do nothing. If you are unable to initiate a commitment yourself, we think it is imperative to have the patient seen by a psychiatrist or taken to an emergency room immediately. You want to document thoroughly to whom you spoke, what you said, and what ultimately happened. This situation presents what is probably the most compelling reason to have a well-developed network. Ideally, you need to have immediate access to emergency-room personnel, more than one psychiatrist, and law-enforcement officers.

As with duty to warn, states interpret laws regulating duty to protect differently. This has resulted in ambiguity of the extent of the therapist's responsibility and liability. As a result of the Tarasoff decision and other cases concerning liability with suicidal and homicidal patients, many therapists have become increasingly conservative in their treatment approaches. In our experience, we have found that most therapists try hard to act in their clients' best interests without being overly self-protective. Yet they feel they must balance this desire to do what is best for the client with the pressures they feel from the threat of litigation. It is unrealistic to expect the limits of liability ever to be completely spelled out for every circumstance. Therefore, we reiterate the importance of therapists' keeping in touch with what is happening in the courts, the professional organizations, and their communities.

☐ Liability Protection

Despite the rise in litigation, a therapist need not practice in fear if he or she applies some common-sense approaches. In general, questions of liability relate to the structure of the practice, with maximum personal liability assumed by those in sole proprietorships and the least exposure by those who are incorporated. The exception is malpractice liability. Although there are no guarantees against susceptibility to a malpractice judgment, practicing in a manner most consistent with the highest standards in the field may deter the possibility of suit. What those standards are can be determined by analyzing information gleaned from a variety of sources. The most obvious source of information and standards is the set of protocols established while the therapist is in training. However, although educational programs do deal with the basics of therapeutic practice, they rarely discuss the specifics of liability. That information is available from discussions with colleagues, professional meetings, continuing-education programs, and the practice audit.

Colleague Discussions, Professional Meetings, and Continuing Education

Once again the maintenance of a network of colleagues and other professional advisors proves necessary. The new independent practitioner can gather information about fees, referral agencies, contact persons within agencies, and standard operating procedures from colleagues. Less official, but no less vital, information, such as quirks within referral agencies, track record of insurance-company claim payments (and the name of the person inside the company who gets things done!), and the status of regulating statutes, is ascertained more easily from colleagues than from any other source.

Professional meetings provide programs on these topics, as well as a wealth of contacts and individuals to serve as "sounding boards" for the practitioner. Long before you read about new ideas and issues in a magazine, journal, or book, they usually are being discussed at professional meetings. Additionally, these meetings often feature invited speakers, sometimes from other professions, who are experts on particularly pressing issues. Your access to such people might be much more limited outside the professional meeting venue.

Continuing-education classes represent another means by which to gather up-to-date information about practice norms and liability (among a number of other topics). Some professional organizations or states mandate a certain amount of continuing education in a given time period. Such required continuing education is minimal at best. Throughout this book, we emphasize the need for independent practitioners to be self-starters. We think such self-starters need to pursue continuing-education opportunities aggressively—above and beyond those that are mandated. Continuing-education classes allow you to update your skills and knowledge about a variety of theoretical and practical concerns from a "real world" vantage point. In addition, continuing-education classes can help you to update yourself on professional organizations' ethics codes. We think it is vitally important not only to be familiar with a code but also to realize that these codes change over time and require regular monitoring. If you take continuing-education classes, you also are in a good position to see gaps in what is being offered, which may present opportunities for you either to "lobby" for a class not currently offered or, depending on your credentials and training, to offer one yourself.

Practice Audits

A practice audit is similar to a financial audit in that it involves a detailed analysis of business and professional practices. The therapist can invite a senior member of the profession to review all business and therapeutic procedures within a given period of time. The consulting colleague evaluates these practices according to the profession's highest standards and ethics and offers criticism. It may be prudent to request that the audit include a written report of the findings and suggestions. The audited therapist should document the steps taken to respond to the criticisms. Good practice mandates obtaining a waiver of confidentiality from each client whose records are reviewed.

A practice audit with an attorney is also an excellent method of preventing lawsuits. As in the collegial audit, the attorney can identify areas of vulnerability and suggest options. (Again, make sure to obtain written waivers of confidentiality if you need to discuss individual cases.) Although it may be costly, the audit can save the practitioner from the devastating losses from a successful lawsuit filed against him or her.

☐ Malpractice Insurance

Declining to purchase malpractice insurance coverage is not the way to save on expenses in your practice. The need for malpractice insurance rises exponentially in partnerships. Sometimes therapists who do some work for or are affiliated with an institution think that they do not need malpractice insurance because the institution is covered. You should check to determine the limits of the institution's coverage and whether or not the specific contractual arrangement you have with the institution allows you to be covered. In addition, it is quite common for the institution, the treating therapist, or the clinical supervisor to be named in a suit. Therefore, we think to be safe you should have individual malpractice insurance even if you also have institutional coverage.

There are different types of malpractice insurance, the two major being occurrence and claims-made coverage. Medical malpractice liability is unique among various forms of liability because of its long-term nature. The statutes of limitations usually are long for medical claims, and sometimes claims are not made until years after an alleged incidence of malpractice. With occurrence coverage, if your policy is in force on the date an alleged malpractice action took place, you are covered. When the claim is made is not important. This type of malpractice insurance works like other types of insurance. For example, it is similar to auto insurance in that if you were responsible for an auto accident while your car is insured, your auto insurance would cover you, even if you were subsequently to allow your coverage to lapse.

With claims-made coverage, on the other hand, both the date of the alleged occurrence and the date on which the claim is made must fall within the period for which you are covered. If you terminate coverage, then a claims-made policy will not cover what happened in the past, even though you may have had coverage at the time. In order to protect yourself in this case, you would have to purchase what is commonly referred to as "tail" coverage—as in, you buy it to "protect your tail." (The technical term is *reporting endorsement*.) A "tail" covers you for claims made after the termination date of your policy for something that allegedly occurred during your previous coverage.

☐ Record Keeping

In order to preclude having their records subpoenaed, some therapists choose not to keep any. We believe that this is, at best, irresponsible. Therapists keep different types of records for different purposes. Some therapists tape postsession reviews that include perceptions, hunches, and reactions that might be misleading were they to be read or heard by others. They then erase the tapes after writing their formal notes. This technique eliminates your susceptibility to having to release, because of court order, any documents other than your formal notes. Taping allows you to ponder the postsession data and document it in a way that triggers the perception or reaction for you but does not incriminate your client to a potential reader.

At the same time we are advising you to keep accurate and complete records, we also caution against indiscriminate release of these records. This is an issue that plagues healthcare institutions and independent practitioners alike. (We are not talking here of court-ordered or otherwise mandated release of information.) Often unauthorized releases take place because of oversight, sloppiness, or false assumptions on the part of the record keeper. Unauthorized release of records has resulted in legal judgments against the therapist responsible. For example, a state supreme court upheld a patient's claim for unauthorized release of medical records, in part because an independent psychiatrist—who had been called in by the patient's employer to evaluate the patient's fitness to return to work— was allowed access to the patient's previous medical records although the patient had never authorized their release. When the psychiatrist had requested the records, no one had thought to question his right to see the records. When faced with a request for records, you should consider the identity of the person requesting them, the content of the records, and your relationships with the subject of the records and other people you have seen in therapy with the subject, in order to decide whether or not you have an obligation to reveal or withhold records. All managed-care companies require record keeping. Most have specific documentation requirements, including intake, treatment planning, evaluation, and request for continued treatment formats. The adage, "If it's not documented, it didn't happen," means, "If you don't document appropriately, you will not get paid."

We have covered many aspects of building your practice throughout this book. We have structured the content to help you successfully define and create a private practice that suits your needs and the needs of your client. One of the things that we like best about private practice is the space it provides to change creatively and grow in a profession that allows for a great deal of individuality and specialization. It is our belief that independent practice for the mental-health professional will continue to flourish in the 21st century. We look forward to joining you in making that happen.

APPENDIX

We offer the following forms used at PCS as examples of the kinds of documents you might find useful in your independent practice. The forms include a new-patient information page given to new clients; a programs form to be used as a treatment guideline that is kept in the patient's chart; an intensive relapse prevention/aftercare plan designed to facilitate a patient's care after he or she was in an intensive therapy program; an acknowledgment and understanding form given to new patients to explain therapy issues of risks and confidentiality, office hours, payment and fees, and insurance procedures; and a release of information form used to authorize a patient's release of confidential information.

PSYCHOLOGICAL COUNSELING SERVICES, LTD.
New Patient Information

Last Name of Patient _____ First Name _____

Patient Street Address _____

City _____ State _____ Zip _____

Home Telephone _____ Work Telephone _____

Birthdate of Patient _____ Sex: M F (Circle One)

Social Security Number of Patient _____

Responsible Party Telephone _____

Billing Address _____

City _____ State _____ Zip _____

Marital Status: (Circle One)
M-Married S-Single Se-Separated D-Divorce W-Widowed

Employer and Address _____

Who Referred You? _____

Who Is Your First Appointment With? _____

Information pertaining to patient's spouse, partner, or guardian

Last Name _____ First Name _____

Street _____

City _____ State _____ Zip _____

Home Telephone _____ Work Telephone _____

Relationship to Patient _____

Birthdate _____ Social Security Number _____

Spouse's Employer and Address _____

Insurance Information

Insurance Company Name _____ Phone No. _____

Insured Party Full Name _____ Relationship to patient _____

Group Name _____ Group ID No. _____

Please provide the receptionist with a copy of your insurance identification card.

1. I hereby authorize the therapist whose name appears on my insurance claim form to furnish my insurance company with any requested information concerning my present treatment.

2. I hereby assign to the therapist whose name appears on my insurance claim form all monies to which I am entitled for psychological expense relative to the services reported on my insurance claim form. I understand that I am financially responsible to said therapist(s) for charges not covered by this assignment.

_____   _____
Insured/Guardian/Responsible Party   Patient   Date

Psychological Counseling Services, Ltd. Programs

Patient Name _____   Referred by _____

Diagnosis _____   Groups _____

Medication _____   F.O.O. Therapy _____

Testing _____   Genogram _____

Prepare/Enrich _____   "Lifeline" Trauma Egg _____

Hypnosis _____   Bibliotherapy _____

Couples Communication _____   Couples Therapy _____

Individual Therapy _____   Family Therapy _____

Edu-therapy _____   Hospitalizations _____

Polygraph _____   Films _____

M.D. _____   Patient's Attorney _____

Other Family Members in Treatment:

_____

_____

PCS Therapists: _____
(primary)

_____

P.C.S. INTENSIVE RELAPSE PREVENTION/AFTERCARE PLAN

INDIVIDUAL
Therapist for: HIS - _____   HER - _____

Freq: _____   Hours: _____   Freq: _____   Hours: _____

COUPLE
Therapist: _____

Freq: _____   Hours: _____

FAMILY
Therapist: _____

Freq: _____   Hours: _____

GROUP
His: FACT _____ COMPULSIVITY _____ CODEPENDENCY _____

ANGER/FORGIVENESS _____ CLERGY _____

Her: FACT _____ COMPULSIVITY _____ CODEPENDENCY _____

ANGER/FORGIVENESS _____ CLERGY _____

Couple: CCP _____ COUPLES _____

SELF HELP GROUPS

SA _____ AA _____ NA _____ CODA _____ OTHER _____

GOALS

1. EMOTIONAL: _____

2. SPIRITUAL : _____

3. INTELLECTUAL: _____

4. PHYSICAL: _____

5. RELATIONAL: _____

SIGNATURES: _____ DATE: _____

Psychological Counseling Services
Acknowledgement and Understanding

Please review this information and ask about anything
you do not fully understand.

Benefits and Emotional Risks:

The majority of individuals and families that obtain behavioral health services benefit from the process. The therapeutic process is generally quite useful, but some risks do exist. As counseling begins, please understand that some experience unwanted feelings, and that examining old issues may produce unhappiness, anger, guilt, or frustration. Important personal decisions are often an outcome of counseling. These are likely to produce new opportunities as well as unique challenges. Sometimes a decision that is positive for one family member will be viewed as negative by another. Don't hesitate to discuss treatment goals, procedures, or your impressions of the services that are being provided.

Confidentiality:

A client's confidentiality is important and legally protected. There are, however, circumstances that impose limitations on a client's right or ability to maintain a privileged communication. When a therapist is out of town, another professional will cover crisis calls and that professional may be advised of your case. If a health care benefit plan is expected to pay for some portion of the cost of services, it is understood that this office may furnish diagnostic and clinical information to insurance companies or medical review organizations in order to obtain reimbursement. In the event that group counseling services are provided, it is further acknowledged that the doctor or practice cannot be held responsible for a breach of confidentiality on the part of a peer group member.

Hours/Availability:
The PCS business office is open from 9 am to 5 pm Monday through Thursday and 9 am to 3 pm on Friday, except for legal holidays. In the event that a crisis occurs and your therapist is unavailable, contact a crisis intervention service, your primary care physician, call 911, or go to the emergency room.

Payment and Fees:
Payment is expected at the time services are rendered. This office accepts cash, checks, Visa or MasterCard.

Insurance:
The patient is responsible for billing their insurance company for reimbursement. We will supply you with a completed charge slip for you to submit.

(*This office will process insurance claims only if you have insurance for which this office or individual therapist is listed as participating. The patient is personally responsible for deductibles, co-payments, coinsurance, non-covered, ineligible, or non-authorized services. Please note that not all therapists may be participating with your plan. Please check with your participating therapist before consultation or treatment with another therapist occurs. Please verify with the bookkeeper/accounts coordinator whether or not your plan is eligible.)

Intensive Programs:
Intensive Program services are to be paid for in full in advance. The patient is responsible for billing the insurance company for reimbursement for Intensive Program services.

Other:
There is a $20 charge on all returned checks. NSF checks must be replaced with cash, certified check, money order, Visa or MasterCard. There is a $3 replacement fee for duplicate charge slips. Delinquent accounts may be referred for collection and credit reporting as well as interest added to balances over 60 days.

Important:
24 hours notice is required if you need to change or cancel an individual therapy appointment or group therapy session or you will be charged the therapist rate for the missed appointment/no show.

I have reviewed this information and agree to these understandings.

_____ _____   _____ _____
Signature of client   Date   Signature of Spouse/other   Date

To assign insurance benefits, please complete:
I authorize the release of medical information necessary to process a claim. I authorize payment of medical benefits to this office or participating provider.

_____ _____
Signature   Date

RELEASE OF INFORMATION

TO: _____

FROM: _____

AUTHORIZATION FOR INFORMATION RELEASE

I authorize _____ and Psychological Counseling Services, Ltd. and the agency or individual listed above to discuss and/or exchange information and/or reports as initialed below. It is understood that this release is granted to assist the staff at each agency/office. It is further understood that this information once obtained, will not be released to any other agency or individual.

PLEASE INITIAL:

_____ Social History/Intake Summary   _____ Treatment Notes

_____ Psychological/Psychiatric Exam   _____ Hospitalization Records

_____ Testing   _____ Thank You For Referral Letter

_____ Other (Please Specify)

I understand that my records are protected under the Federal Confidentiality Regulations and cannot be released or disclosed without my written permission unless otherwise provided for in the law. I also understand that I may revoke this consent at any time except to the extent that action has been taken in reliance thereon.

DATE: _____   _____
                        Signature of Self, Parent or Guardian

                        _____
                        Signature of Witness

SUGGESTED READINGS

Butcher, J. N. (1990). *Use of the MMPI-2 in treatment planning.* New York: Oxford University Press.

Butcher, J. N. (Ed.). (1997). *Personality assessment in managed health care: Using the MMPI-2 in treatment planning.* New York: Oxford University Press.

Poynter, W. L. (1998). *The textbook of behavioral managed care: From concept through management.* Philadelphia, PA: Brunner/Mazel Publishers.

Small Business Administration. *Directory of business development publications, Form SBA 115 A-M.* Washington, DC: U.S. Government Printing Office.

Sperry, L. S. (1996). *Corporate therapy and consulting.* Philadelphia, PA: Brunner/Mazel Publishers.

Spitz, H. I. (1995). *Group psychotherapy and managed mental health care: A clinical guide for providers.* Philadelphia, PA: Brunner/Mazel Publishers.

INDEX

CPSIA information can be obtained
at www.ICGtesting.com
Printed in the USA
FFHW011826041218
49749488-54195FF